Nevada

NEVADA BY ROAD

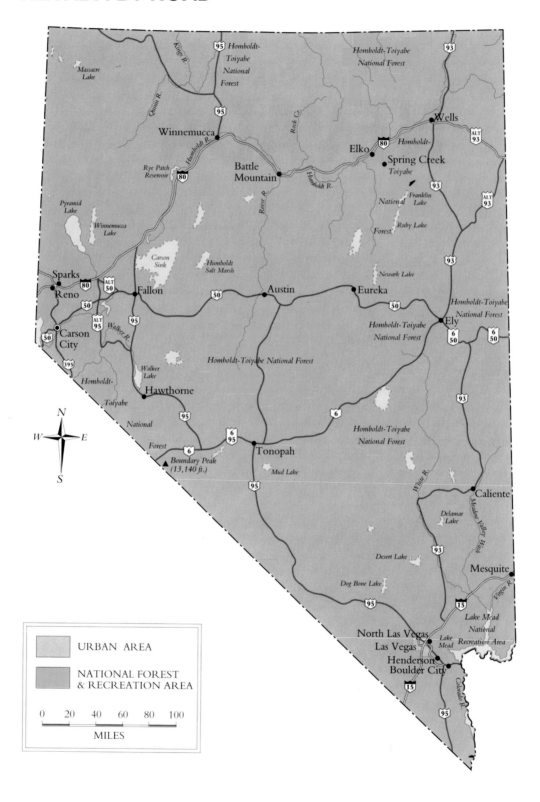

Celebrate the States

Nevada

Rebecca Stefoff

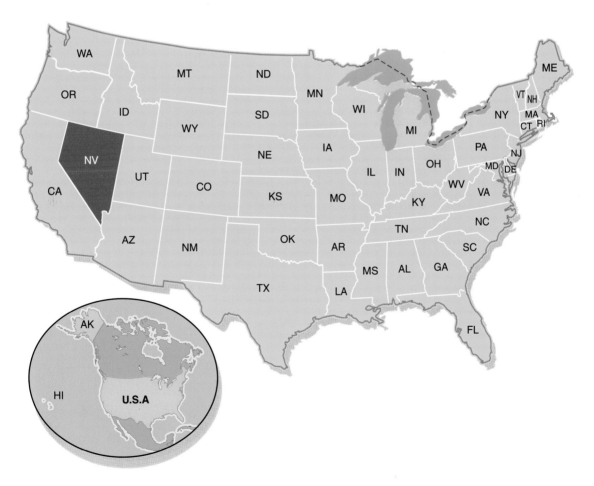

mc Marshall Cavendish
Benchmark
New York

Other Marshall Cavendish Offices:
Marshall Cavendish Ltd. 5th Floor, 32-38 Saffron Hill, London EC1N 8 FH, UK • Marshall Cavendish International (Asia)
Private Limited, 1 New Industrial Road, Singapore 536196 • Marshall Cavendish International (Thailand) Co Ltd. 253 Asoke,
12th Flr, Sukhumvit 21 Road, Klongtoey Nua, Wattana, Bangkok 10110, Thailand • Marshall Cavendish (Malaysia) Sdn Bhd,
Times Subang, Lot 46, Subang Hi-Tech Industrial Park, Batu Tiga, 40000 Shah Alam, Selangor Darul Ehsan, Malaysia

Marshall Cavendish is a trademark of Times Publishing Limited

All websites were available and accurate when this book was sent to press.

Library of Congress Cataloging-in-Publication Data
Stefoff, Rebecca.
Nevada / by Rebecca Stefoff.—2nd ed.
p. cm. — (Celebrate the states)
Summary: "Provides comprehensive information on the geography, history, wildlife, governmental structure,
economy, cultural diversity, peoples, religion, and landmarks of Nevada"—Provided by publisher.
Includes bibliographical references and index.
ISBN 978-0-7614-4728-3
1. Nevada—Juvenile literature. I. Title.

F841.3.S72 2011
979.3—dc22
2009007137

Editor: Christine Florie
Co-Editor: Denise Pangia
Publisher: Michelle Bisson
Art Director: Anahid Hamparian
Series Designer: Adam Mietlowski

Photo research and layout by Marshall Cavendish International (Asia) Private Limited—
Thomas Khoo, Benson Tan and Gu Jing

Cover photo by Photolibrary

The photographs in this book are used by permission and through the courtesy of: *Alt. TYPE / Reuters*: 69, 119; *Corbis*: 15, 39,
49, 52, 54, 68, 86, 88, 121, 124, 125, 126, 127, 128; *Getty Images*: 17, 21, 28, 72, 117, 118, 123; *National Geographic Image
Collection*: 61, 112, 122; *North Wind Picture Archives*: 33, 38, 42, 46; *Photolibrary*: back cover; 13, 14, 20, 24, 30, 32, 56, 70,
75, 81, 83, 85, 94, 97, 99, 101, 103, 105, 109, 115, 130, 132, 135, 136; *Photolibrary / Alamy*: 8, 10, 18, 34, 59, 64, 78, 90, 92,
98, 100, 106, 131, 133, 134; *Topfoto*: 66, 120, 129.

Printed in Malaysia
1 3 5 6 4 2

Contents

Nevada Is . . .

Nevada is Las Vegas, a city built on gambling and famous for its nightlife and bright lights.

"Las Vegas looks the way you'd imagine heaven must look at night."
—writer Chuck Palahniuk, *Invisible Monsters*, 1999

"Where else can you go in a few short blocks and see the Eiffel Tower, pyramids, a castle, and erupting volcanoes?"
—Burton Cohen, retired casino executive, 1999

"[Las Vegas is] a figment of its own imagination, the Elvis Presley of American cities."
—librarian Kevin Starr

But Nevada is also huge stretches of rugged, almost empty land.

"Maybe Las Vegas was never supposed to become a real city, or Nevada a real state. . . . We're assaulted almost daily with bad news about this inhospitable, hardscrabble desert we call home."
—Steve Sebelius, *Las Vegas CityLife*, July 17, 2008

"Here's what Nevada really is: not Las Vegas, not Reno, just miles and miles of road, up through a pass and down into the flatland over and over again, hardly any trees, only a few little towns, just land. Sometimes, when I'm driving at night, I'll pass hundreds of cattle on the road, maybe a few deer, and just two or three cars or trucks all night long. Sometimes when I'm passing through in the daytime I look at those mountains and think to myself that I'd like to get out of the truck and see what's behind them someday."
—R. J. Oates, long-haul trucker

Nevada has attracted many different kinds of settlers, from the stubbornly independent adventurers of the early days to the suburban homesteaders of the state's new land rush.

"With the vastness of the desert made glorious by the morning sun; the vivid glory of magnificent mountains enclosing the valley on all sides . . . the train bumped slowly along and at last came to a stop near an old passenger coach on a little spur, on which was nailed a piece of board on which was painted the magic name 'Las Vegas.'"
—C. P. Squires, who came to Nevada from California in 1905

"Nevada today is a strange combination of a sophisticated society and a mining frontier; while there have been liberal attitudes toward gambling and divorce, powerful conservative elements dominate the state's politics."
—Nevada historian Russell R. Elliott

American Indians have lived in Nevada for thousands of years, adapting their ways of life to the resources it offered. European explorers and American pioneers, however, saw Nevada as a dry and dangerous obstacle to be crossed. Only when the land revealed its mineral riches did settlers come to Nevada. Things had changed a lot by the dawn of the twenty-first century, when Nevada was America's fastest-growing state. Although the population boom shapes the state's economic and political future, the influences of the land's pioneer past and of the land itself remain strong.

Chapter One

Sagebrush and Sand

The "Sagebrush State" is one of Nevada's nicknames. Another is the "Silver State." Together the names reflect the two sides of this western state. Silver is woven through Nevada's past and its present. The fabulous wealth of silver mines drew miners and settlers to the region in the nineteenth century. Today silver stands for money—the millions of coins that clatter endlessly through glittering, clanging slot machines, the symbol of the state's famous gambling industry.

Sagebrush represents a very different Nevada, a place of windswept, wide-open spaces. The silvery gray-green leaves of this hardy shrub, sprinkled with yellow flowers in late summer, give the landscape its characteristic color and fill the air with a clean, sharp fragrance after summer rainstorms. Sagebrush is a reminder that in spite of the urban glamour of Las Vegas, the state of Nevada belongs to the American West.

THE GREAT BASIN

Nevada is shaped like a giant wedge driven between the Rocky Mountains and the Sierra Nevada, the California mountain range that rises across

Spikey yucca plants dot the rugged landscape of the Red Rock Canyon National Conservation Area, just outside of Las Vegas.

Nevada's western border. Nevada is bordered by Oregon and Idaho in the north, Utah in the east, Arizona in the southeast, and California in the west.

Like the Sierra Nevada, the state got its name from *nevada*, a Spanish word meaning "snowcapped." The name is a little misleading though. Nevada does have some towering, snow-tipped peaks, but the state consists mostly of dry semidesert and low, dusty mountain ranges. Its highest point is 13,140-foot Boundary Peak, which straddles the Nevada–California border. On the opposite side of the state, not far from the Utah border, stands Wheeler Peak, Nevada's second-highest mountain at 13,063 feet. Many other peaks around the state rise above 10,000 feet.

Wheeler Peak, standing at 13,063 feet, towers above a high valley in Great Basin National Park.

Most of Nevada lies within a large geographic region that extends into Utah, Idaho, Oregon, and southern California. In the nineteenth century, explorer John Charles Frémont named this region the Great Basin because it is like an immense basin, or bowl, between the Rocky Mountain ranges and the Sierra Nevada, with all of its streams flowing inward rather than toward the sea. Nevada forms by far the largest portion of the Great Basin.

The Great Basin is made up of about one hundred smaller basins or flatlands separated by rows of mountain ranges that run north–south. Geographer Clarence Dutton compared these ranges to "an army of caterpillars marching toward Mexico." Nearly all of Nevada is covered with these caterpillar ranges. The ranges are close together. As the road climbs to the crest of a pass through one range, you can gaze ahead to see it crossing the level basin below and then rising up to the next crest. In summer the landscape seems to shimmer with heat, haze, and dust.

Nevada's northeastern corner lies outside the Great Basin. This part of Nevada resembles the high, windy plains of eastern Oregon and southern Idaho. The Bruneau, Jarbidge, and Owyhee rivers rise in this part of the state and flow north to join the Snake River beyond Nevada's boundaries.

The southeastern point of Nevada, a hot desert region of sand and sunbaked red rock, also falls outside the Great Basin. The western edge of the point, along the California border, lies next to Death Valley, the lowest-lying and hottest place in the United States. Although most of Death Valley National Park is within California, a corner of the park reaches into Nevada's Amargosa Desert. Most of Nevada's point lies within the Mojave Desert, which extends into California on the west,

LAND AND WATER

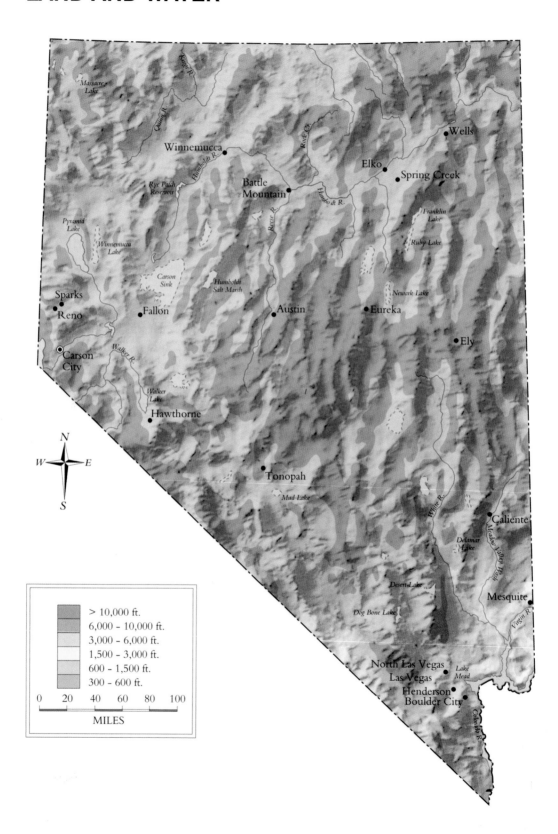

Massacre Lake

Quinn R.

King R.

Winnemucca

Rye Patch Reservoir

Humboldt R.

Battle Mountain

Rock Cr.

Wells

Elko

Spring Creek

Humboldt R.

Franklin Lake

Ruby Lake

Pyramid Lake

Winnemucca Lake

Reese R.

Carson Sink

Humboldt Salt Marsh

Newark Lake

Sparks

Reno

Fallon

Austin

Eureka

Ely

Carson City

Walker R.

Walker Lake

Hawthorne

N
W E
S

Tonopah

Mud Lake

White R.

Caliente

Delamar Lake

Meadow Valley Wash

Desert Lake

Dog Bone Lake

Mesquite

Virgin R.

North Las Vegas

Lake Mead

Las Vegas

Henderson

Boulder City

Colorado R.

> 10,000 ft.
6,000 – 10,000 ft.
3,000 – 6,000 ft.
1,500 – 3,000 ft.
600 – 1,500 ft.
300 – 600 ft.

0   20   40   60   80   100

MILES

Utah on the northeast, and Arizona on the east. The Muddy and Virgin rivers flow south through the Nevada portion of the Mojave and empty into the Colorado River. The Colorado, which defines Nevada's border with Arizona, drains into the Gulf of California, an arm of the Pacific Ocean.

Nevada's four largest rivers, however, drain into the Great Basin. The Truckee flows down from the Sierra Nevada into Pyramid Lake, near the state's western border. The Walker flows into Walker Lake, farther south. The Humboldt and Carson rivers flow into sinks—marshy, low-lying depressions. Most of Nevada's smaller rivers and streams end in sinks or in playas, which are large stretches of dry, cracked clay.

Encompassing 125,000 acres makes Pyramid Lake one of the largest natural lakes in Nevada.

MONSTERS FROM ANCIENT WATERS

Nevada wasn't always dry. During the last Ice Age, which ended about 11,000 years ago, its higher mountain ranges were covered with sheets of ice. Rivers draining from this ice formed large lakes. Lahontan, Nevada's largest Ice Age lake, once covered 8,450 square miles of western Nevada. For thousands of years, though, Lake Lahontan has been drying up. All that remains today are Pyramid and Walker lakes, Humboldt and Carson sinks, dozens of playas, and the Black Rock, Smoke Creek, and Granite Creek deserts, which used to be the bottom of the lake.

Before there were lakes, there was the sea. Millions of years ago, Nevada was covered by warm, shallow seas filled with life. The remains of plants and animals fell to the sea bottom, were covered with sand and mud, and over long ages became fossils. Among the creatures preserved beneath Nevada's ancient seas were ichthyosaurs (below), 25-foot-long reptiles with large eyes, long snouts, and sharp teeth. Nevada has made this impressive hunter its official state fossil.

Once a lake bed, the Black Rock Desert is now a sea of dry, cracked clay.

Some parts of the state, such as the Black Rock Desert in the northwestern corner, have huge playas. For miles, the earth looks like a giant jigsaw puzzle cut into pieces as much as 1 foot thick. Many of the state's waterways are seasonal. They flow freely in winter and spring but dry up completely by summer's end.

The largest natural lake in the state is Pyramid, named for an island on the lake's eastern shore that reminded explorer Frémont of the pyramids of Egypt. Lake Tahoe, a magnificent blue gem nestled in the foothills of the Sierra Nevada, is larger, but part of it lies in California. Largest of all is Lake Mead, an artificial reservoir created by the damming of the Colorado River.

HOT AND DRY

Drought, which means a prolonged dry period, is becoming an unwelcome new reality in Nevada and other parts of the American West. During the first years of the twenty-first century, temperatures were higher and rainfall was lower than in previous years. Scientists now know that the twentieth century—the period when the West was developed and population centers grew—was an unusually wet period in the history of the region's climate. The climate is now swinging back toward its long-term "normal," which means that even though some years are likely to be wetter and cooler than others, Nevada is expected to remain hotter and drier, on average, than it was during the last century.

Nevada has a semidesert climate. Only patches of the state are true desert, expanses of bare rock or sand with few plants. In these deserts, precipitation—moisture that falls as rain or snow—may total less than 5 inches per year. Over the entire state, average yearly precipitation is 7 inches, making Nevada the driest state in the nation. The higher mountains, which receive heavy snowfall, are the wettest parts of the state.

Nevada's storms can be fierce. Winter blizzards are rare, but occasionally they shut down highways and cut off mountain towns for days at a time. Even worse are the summer thunderstorms. These lightning-wracked downpours may last less than half an hour but wipe out roads, bridges—and, in some tragic cases, unlucky campers or hikers caught in canyons as flash floods roar down upon them.

The opposite of storm, of course, is sunshine. Nevada has plenty of sunny days. "The sun is this place's most precious resource," says a retired accountant from Connecticut who moved to the outskirts of Las Vegas to enjoy cloudless skies on the golf course. He has many chances to enjoy that resource—Las Vegas has up to 320 sunny days a year.

Summer lightning strikes can set trees ablaze, causing wildfires in forested areas of the state.

But with all that sunshine comes heat. In the summer it's not unusual for Nevada to record the nation's highest temperatures, up to 125 degrees Fahrenheit in the southern tip of the state. Winter temperatures in the northern mountains have plummeted as low as −50 °F, recorded at San Jacinto in 1937.

Nevada is famous for large temperature shifts during a single day. Especially in late spring and early fall, daytime highs and lows may be 50 degrees apart. People who sweltered in shorts and T-shirts all afternoon may find themselves shivering in sweaters as soon as the sun goes down.

Sagebrush is Nevada's state flower, and for good reason. It flourishes in semidesert conditions and covers a fifth of the state. In the south, creosote and mesquite bushes are common. Yucca plants, which produce white flowers on spikes, grow in the warmer parts of the state, as do their larger and shaggier cousins, Joshua trees. Nevada has more than two dozen kinds of cacti, some of which produce surprisingly colorful and delicate blossoms among their spines.

The prickly pear cactus, which produces colorful blossoms, gives way to luscious, edible fruits.

Large expanses of Nevada are treeless, except where home owners have planted shade trees or decorative palm trees. Forest covers only about 12 percent of the state. Piñon and juniper trees carpet the lower mountain slopes. Higher up, pines and firs flourish. High forests in the eastern and southern parts of the state may also include bristlecone pines. These tough, low-growing trees are among the world's longest-living plants—some are thousands of years old. Throughout the state, streams are bordered by tangles of chokecherry, alder, willow, and cottonwood trees whose leaves turn bright yellow in the fall.

Dozens of species of birds make their home in Nevada—or pass through it. Hundreds of thousands of ducks and geese stop in western Nevada's lakes and streams while migrating. So do pelicans. You may associate these big-billed birds with ocean beaches and harbors, but the American white pelican breeds on the islands of Pyramid Lake. Golden and bald eagles, owls, falcons, and songbirds such as the mountain bluebird also make their home in the state. Birds of the Mojave are found in the southern part of the state. Among them are roadrunners, cactus wrens, and burrowing owls—small, long-legged owls that live in tunnels beneath the desert surface.

The desert of the south also has numerous reptiles. Desert iguanas, collared lizards, whiptail lizards, and the large, stumpy-tailed lizards known as chuckwallas may be spotted soaking up the sun on warm rocks. Slow-moving desert tortoises—Nevada's state reptile—and sidewinder snakes also live in the Mojave. King snakes, gopher snakes, and rattlesnakes live in other parts of the state, as do horned lizards and fence lizards. In all, Nevada has several dozen kinds of lizards. They may

The chuckwalla can often be found on boulder-covered slopes at elevations up to 4,500 feet.

look like small dinosaurs, but these shy creatures are harmless—except for the black-and-orange Gila monster. Its bite is mildly poisonous, but it would much rather avoid you than bite you.

The mule deer is the most common large wild animal in Nevada, but the state also has herds of bighorn sheep, pronghorn antelope, and elk. Coyotes are the most common predators. Bobcats and cougars, or mountain lions, live in the forested areas, and black bears are sometimes seen there as well. Smaller kinds of wildlife abound in Nevada. Rabbits are most common, but there are also badgers, red foxes, minks, muskrats, beavers, raccoons, and porcupines.

Nevada is home to a large population of wild burros and mustangs. These animals are the descendants of horses and donkeys introduced to the Americas by the Spaniards in the sixteenth century. Animals that ran away or were abandoned adapted to life in the wilderness.

In the Spring Mountains, north of Las Vegas, bands of wild mustangs roam free.

Now, generations later, they are wild. Many visitors to Nevada are thrilled to catch a glimpse of a mustang galloping across the plain with its mane streaming in the wind, but some folks have greater admiration for the tough, sturdy burros. "These little burros may not look as romantic as wild horses," says a ranger at Nevada's Red Rock Canyon National Conservation Area, "but they are smart, nimble, very efficient grazers. They are supremely well adapted to life in this environment." If you drive along the back roads of southern Nevada, look for light-colored patches about knee-high in the fields. Those patches are the pale muzzles of burros, who will raise their heads, ears erect, to watch you pass.

ENDANGERED AND PROTECTED

Under the federal Endangered Species Act (ESA), the U.S. government recognizes some species as endangered, which means that they are likely to become extinct unless they and their habitats are protected by law. The federal list of endangered species in Nevada contains one insect (a butterfly called the Carson wandering skipper), two plants (steamboat buckwheat and Amargosa niterwort), seventeen fish, and five birds. Of the birds, only the Yuma clapper rail and the southwestern willow flycatcher are full-time Nevada residents.

A number of other species, however, are classified by the federal government as threatened, which means that they are at risk of becoming endangered. One of these species is Nevada's state reptile, the desert tortoise. People are the biggest threat to the tortoise's survival in the wild. Collectors take desert tortoises to be sold as pets, even though it is illegal to own them without special licenses. Human development that turns wild land into malls and housing developments threatens the tortoise's habitat. In addition, tortoises are killed by cars and trucks as they cross roads.

Wildlife researchers think that some other plant and animal species in Nevada should be included in the endangered and threatened list. Until the federal government decides whether these species deserve protection, it classifies them as candidates. Among them are three species of toads and frogs, a bird called the yellow-billed cuckoo, and five plants.

One of Nevada's most gravely endangered species is a tiny fish, about three-quarters of an inch long when fully grown, called the Devils Hole pupfish. It is native to just one place in the world—Devils Hole, a deep pool of hot water that wells up in a cave in the Amargosa Desert. There the fish feed on algae that grows on a limestone shelf in the water, and they also deposit their eggs on the shelf. Devils Hole lies within a Nevada wildlife refuge but is officially part of Death Valley National Park. The site is protected because the pupfish is extremely rare.

The saga of the Devils Hole pupfish shows the challenges that face endangered species. Not only have these tiny fish been at the center of court battles, but the scientists who are working to protect them are struggling to understand their life cycle and breeding habits. The protection of the pupfish began in 1952, when Death Valley National Park was created. In 1967 the pupfish were given endangered species status, which kicked off a legal battle.

The law protects the habitats of endangered species as well as the plants and animals themselves, which meant that the protection given to the pupfish also extended to Devils Hole itself. Farming operations in the area, however, were drawing water to irrigate their fields from

The Devils Hole pupfish population resides in southern Nevada in a single small pool at the bottom of a limestone cave.

the same underground water sources that fill Devils Hole. When agricultural activities threatened to lower the water level in Devils Hole and possibly kill the pupfish, environmentalists went to court. The issue divided Nevadans. Some of them felt that humans must make some sacrifices to allow other species to survive, while others argued that an obscure fish should not stand in the way of human activities such as raising crops. People drove around with "Save the Pupfish" and "Kill the Pupfish" bumper stickers.

The battle over the pupfish went all the way to the U.S. Supreme Court, which in 1976 ruled to place limits on the agricultural use of water in order to preserve the Devils Hole habitat. But the favorable ruling did not mean that the pupfish's troubles were over. The population of Devils Hole, normally about five hundred fish, dropped in the late twentieth and early twenty-first centuries to a low of thirty-eight in 2006. Although pupfish are now being bred in artificial habitats called refugia, in case the native population dies out, scientists were glad to report in 2008 that divers venturing into Devils Hole had counted 126 fish. Experts are now investigating the place of the pupfish in the Devils Hole ecosystem. "We still have a long ways to go to fully understanding this system," says David Ek of the National Park Service.

WATER WOES

The Devils Hole pupfish is not the only inhabitant of Nevada that has known the trouble of water shortages. Everyone in the state may soon be feeling drier than usual. Like other states in the American Southwest, Nevada faces a future in which water shortages may grow more severe.

Providing water to thirsty cities, towns, farms, and wildlife is likely to be the state's biggest environmental challenge in the coming decades.

Drought is part of the water problem. The other part is growth. Between 2000 and 2006, Nevada's population increased by almost 25 percent. This rapid population growth, especially in Las Vegas, brought increased demand for water: for drinking, for watering lawns and washing cars and filling swimming pools, and for farming. The amount of available water, unfortunately, did not go up. In fact, it went down.

Nevada has two sources of water. One is groundwater, natural underground reserves of water. In recent decades, groundwater levels have fallen because the water has been used far faster than it can be restored through rainfall. The state's other main source of water is the Colorado River. Nevada is one of seven states that share the Colorado's water under an agreement that dates from the 1920s (a small share also goes to Mexico under an international treaty). The amount of water flowing through the Colorado River has been steadily dropping, however, because of drought in the West and because people keep taking more water out of the river system.

By 2007 the level of the Colorado River was lower than it had been in the eighty-five years since measurements began. Global warming will only make things worse. Environmental engineer Bradley Udall told the U.S. Congress in 2007 that the region around the Colorado River was 2 °F warmer, on average, than in 1976. Rising temperatures in the future may cause more water to evaporate into the air, further reducing the supply.

Nevada's portion of the Colorado River is the smallest among the seven states that share the water, although it has made a deal with Arizona to buy some of that state's share. Both states, as well as southern California and northern Mexico, draw Colorado River water from Lake Mead, a vast artificial reservoir. By 2007 the water level had fallen so much that the lake was only 49 percent full. Afraid that the lake's surface may drop below the intake pipes that draw water out of the lake and send it to homes, businesses, and farms, the Southern Nevada Water Authority is drilling new pipes, closer to the bottom of Lake Mead, to avoid being left high and dry. Piping water to southern Nevada from the northern part of the state is another possibility—although it is not popular in northern Nevada.

To save water, southern Nevada officials have enacted laws such as banning the construction of new artificial lakes in the Las Vegas area. Many of the big water users—the golf courses and the casinos with artificial lakes and waterfalls—already practice conservation, recycling and reusing their water. Home owners are less efficient. Water authorities estimate that of all the water used in private residences, less than one-third is used inside the homes. Most residential water is used for washing cars and watering lawns.

"The single biggest use of water when the temperature soars here is people watering their lawns," says one Las Vegas official. "And people overwater profusely." To cut back on the amount of water that is wasted on unnecessary or inefficient lawn care, water managers encourage xeriscaping, or dry landscaping, designing yards with sand, rocks,

The white band around Lake Mead shows how far the water level has fallen since its high point in 1983.

and drought-resistant plants native to the region. This approach to yard design, however, has been slow to catch on.

Nevada water manager Pat Mulroy says, "We have an exploding human population, and we have a shrinking clean-water supply. Those are on colliding paths. This is not just a Las Vegas issue." She adds, "The people who move to the West today need to realize they're moving into a desert. If they want to live in a desert, they have to adapt to a desert lifestyle." That lifestyle may include laws that limit lawn watering and car washing, as well as higher fees for water use. Yet if Las Vegas and Nevada are among the first parts of the country to bear the brunt of water shortages, perhaps they will also be pioneers in water conservation.

Chapter Two

The Heart of the Golden West

Nevada's state song ends: "Right in the heart of the golden west/Home means Nevada to me." Nevada has been golden in various ways. To its first inhabitants, it was a sun-bathed landscape painted in earthen colors. Later, Nevada drew prospectors with the lure of buried gold and silver. Today the state's golden allure includes neon lights and big dreams of casino winnings.

PREHISTORIC PEOPLE

Most scientists think that the first Americans came from Asia thousands of years ago, during the Ice Age, when ocean levels were lower and a land bridge linked Siberia in northeastern Asia to Alaska. In time the descendants of these migrants spread out across the Americas. By 12,000 years ago, hunting people called Paleo-Indians were living

Nineteenth-century prospectors searched for gold by washing streambed gravel in a simple device called a cradle, which was rocked from side to side.

Early hunters in Nevada tackled big game animals, such as mammoths, which are now extinct.

in Nevada. Some Paleo-Indians lived in caves along Lake Lahontan, where stone dart points, fishing nets, and baskets have been found. Elsewhere in Nevada, archaeologists have found stone spear points that Paleo-Indians used to hunt mammoths—huge, shaggy, elephant-like creatures that are now extinct.

Over the centuries the weather grew drier and hotter. Big game became scarce, and people began hunting smaller prey such as tortoises, rabbits, and squirrels.

Around 300 BCE the Anasazi culture appeared in the Moapa Valley in southeastern Nevada. At first the Anasazi lived in pits roofed with sticks and mud, but by about 700 CE they were building structures of sun-dried clay brick. The main Anasazi community, home to between 1,000 and 20,000 people, consisted of pit houses, caves, and large brick structures called pueblos, some with as many as a hundred rooms. The Anasazi were also master potters and farmers.

Sometime after 1150 the Anasazi disappeared from Nevada. Drought or warfare may have driven them east to Arizona and New Mexico. In the 1920s their abandoned city was discovered and

The Anasazi, also called Ancestral Puebloans, built dwellings of many rooms and levels.

named Pueblo Grande de Nevada. Today it is more often called the Lost City. After Hoover Dam was built to harness the waters of the Colorado River in 1936, the rising waters of Lake Mead covered the city.

RECORDED IN ROCK

Nevada's early inhabitants left records of their presence in the form of petroglyphs, which are images and symbols chipped or scratched into rock. Not just in Nevada but all across the West, these symbols appear on large boulders and on the rock walls of canyons, caves, and cliffs.

Some petroglyphs are tiny, while others are huge. Some of the images are dozens of feet from the ground. Archaeologists who have studied the petroglyphs think that the people who carved the highest images stood on ladders made of tree trunks or limbs.

Hundreds of petroglyphs are scattered across Nevada's landscape. Two places with large collections of these ancient markings are the Grimes Point Petroglyph Trail in the west-central part of the state, and Valley of Fire State Park east of Las Vegas. The Grimes Point path was declared a national recreation trail in 1978. It winds through a boulder garden of large stones bearing hundreds of images such as circles, lines, human figures, and animals. At Valley of Fire the prehistoric images are concentrated in Petroglyph Canyon and on Atlatl Rock. The canyon is a narrow, winding gorge whose walls are lined with images. The rock is a huge boulder ornamented with circles, lines, human and animal figures, and shapes that may represent trees.

The Anasazi petroglyphs on Atlatl Rock in the Valley of Fire State Park are visible to passersby, about 40 to 60 feet above the ground.

How old are the petroglyphs? Attaching a firm date to these rock-carved symbols is impossible, but scientists have made estimates based on the weathering of the rock surfaces and the overlapping of different artistic styles. Some experts have dated the Grimes Point petroglyphs to about six thousand years old. The Valley of Fire petroglyphs are generally thought to be more recent, perhaps made by the Anasazi or other peoples who lived in the area during the past several thousand years. Researchers who have studied rock art believe that over thousands of years of prehistory, many different groups of people made petroglyphs.

Petroglyphs' meanings are as unknown as their ages and their makers' identities. No one—not even modern American Indians—can offer more than guesses about what these symbols meant to the prehistoric people who made them. The petroglyphs may have had religious significance, or recorded important events, or marked the way to sites such as good hunting grounds or meeting places. Or they may have had no purpose beyond expressing their makers' creativity. Although the petroglyphs left in rock by America's early inhabitants speak to us across a gulf of thousands of years, we do not know what they are saying.

AMERICAN INDIANS

After the Anasazi left, other American-Indian peoples flourished in Nevada. The four major groups were the Northern Paiutes in the western part of the state, the Shoshones in eastern and central Nevada, the Southern Paiutes in the southeastern corner, and the Washoes around Lake Tahoe.

These American Indians knew how to take advantage of the resources offered by their sometimes harsh environment. They gathered wild foods such as pine nuts, raspberries, wild carrots, and seeds that they pounded into a flour to thicken their soups. In the mountains they hunted antelopes and bighorn sheep. Lower down, they took rabbits and other small game, often using clever traps to capture the animals.

HOW THE MOTH CAUGHT FIRE IN HIS WINGS

The Paiutes have many traditional legends that tell how things came to be the way they are. This story describes the origin of the red-winged moth.

A wicked magician named Un-nu-pit loved fire so much that he slept on hot coals. Un-nu-pit made all the trouble in the world.

Un-nu-pit had many warriors and dancers who went out into the world to do his bidding. One of them was named Ne-ab. One night Ne-ab flew to a Paiute camp. Fluttering his black wings like a bat, he danced in and out of the Paiutes' firelight, teasing the young people and trying to make them chase him so that they would run into the fire. But Ne-ab was overcome by the beautiful eyes of the young maidens around the fire, and he fell into the flames, which scorched and killed him.

Then Un-nu-pit raised up Ne-ab, wrapped him in a silky soft blanket, and hid him safely away all through the long winter. The following spring, the maidens in the Paiute camp remembered the dancer who had once visited them. They missed his antics. Then a winged being fluttered into the firelight. It was Ne-ab, but he was no longer black. His body and wings were velvety gray, like the ashes of an old fire, but the underside of his wings flowed like flame as he danced before the maidens.

Wooden or stuffed decoys lured waterfowl to ponds where they could be taken with nets or spears. The people of the Great Basin also knew which insects were edible and used them as an important source of protein. Grasshoppers, for example, were a valuable resource.

Nevada's Indians traveled from place to place with the seasons, moving from one food source to another. They usually wintered in sheltered valleys, where they built snug pit houses. During the rest of the year they lived in shelters of grass or reed laid across pole frameworks. They wore clothing of deerskin or pounded sagebrush bark. Rabbit skin blankets were prized possessions.

The Indians usually lived in small bands, but they would gather in larger groups for rabbit hunts or pine-nut harvests. These would be times of celebration, with dancing, games, and gambling—which existed in Nevada long before the first casino was built.

PASSING THROUGH

After Spain conquered Mexico in the early sixteenth century, the Spaniards claimed a large territory north of Mexico, from Texas to California. For several hundred years, however, Spain showed no interest in Nevada. Not until 1776 did someone from Spanish Mexico enter Nevada. While looking for a route from Santa Fe, New Mexico, to Monterey, California, Father Francisco Garcés possibly passed through Nevada's southern tip. After that first visit, Spain and Mexico again left Nevada alone. In the 1840s, after the Mexican War, the United States gained ownership of Nevada. But even before that time a number of American and British adventurers were active in Nevada.

The first to appear were the fur trappers and traders, sometimes called mountain men. They were looking for beaver, whose smooth, waterproof fur was in great demand for hats and coats. Two of the most widely traveled mountain men were Peter Skene Ogden, who worked for the British, and Jedediah Smith, an American. In the 1820s Ogden trapped and explored in northeastern Nevada, along the Humboldt River, and around Walker Lake. Smith arrived in Nevada in 1826, leading a band of trappers from Utah. They crossed the southern tip of Nevada to California and then returned eastward, heading across central Nevada and suffering dreadful hardships in the

Mountain men hauled loads of valuable furs out of the West.

waterless Great Basin. Smith is believed to be the first white person to cross Nevada. He was the first to report the conditions deep inside the Great Basin. Explorer John Charles Frémont followed in the 1840s, leading several expeditions that mapped the Great Basin, including parts of Nevada.

Beginning in the 1840s, thousands of Americans migrated west along the wagon routes called the Oregon and California trails. Those bound for the Pacific Northwest did not usually enter Nevada, but many of those bound for California crossed Nevada, reaching California through passes in the Sierra Nevada. To these early travelers, Nevada was just an obstacle, something to get through on the way to something better. This was even more true after gold was discovered in California in 1848. Americans passed through Nevada, cursing its dust and heat, on their way to the California goldfields. Within a few years, however, Nevada would become a destination in its own right.

THE COMSTOCK LODE

In 1850 Congress created the Utah Territory, which included much of present-day Nevada. The Mormons, a religious group who had settled Utah, founded a few settlements in the Carson Valley. They even discovered small amounts of gold east of Lake Tahoe.

In 1859 miners struck gold there, at a place they called Gold Hill. A few months later a pair of prospectors made a startling discovery nearby. Seeing gold flecks in the sand of a spring, they dug deeper and found a ledge of solid gold. A third miner, Henry Tompkins Paige Comstock, immediately claimed that he owned the land. Although everyone in the area regarded Comstock as lazy and untrustworthy, he managed to get a share of the claim.

Henry Tompkins Paige Comstock's name was given to a rich vein of gold and silver.

The gold ledge was part of an enormous vein of precious metal running through the hills. This fabulous treasure, soon known as the Comstock Lode, kicked off a new gold rush. At first, no one realized just how large the Comstock was. Nor did they recognize what it held.

But after miners complained about the blue clay that was constantly in their way, experts discovered that the clay was silver ore, and that the Comstock Lode was even richer in silver than in gold. A California paper published the news, and the rush was on.

Tent camps called Gold Hill and Silver City sprang up as miners rushed across the Sierra Nevada to the region they had passed through so impatiently just a few years before. The biggest community was named Virginia City. The winter of 1859–1860 was a bitter time on the Comstock. Most miners did not bring enough food with them, and farms and ranches were scarce in the region. Once snow had closed the Sierra Nevada passes, it was almost impossible to bring supplies from California. Those who had supplies could sell them for astonishing prices—sacks of flour went for $885 each. As in other gold rushes, most of the people who made fortunes were not the hopeful miners but the enterprising men and women who provided them with goods and entertainment.

STATEHOOD

The inrush of people to Virginia City and the mines of western Nevada led to lawlessness, confusion, and fights over mining claims. The Utah officials, far away in Salt Lake City, had a hard time governing their wild frontier territory.

Trouble also arose with the American Indians, who resented the Comstockers for killing all the game and cutting down the trees that produced pine nuts, a staple of their diet. Although the Paiute leader Winnemucca urged the Indians to remain peaceful, fighting broke out after white men kidnapped two Paiute girls in the spring of 1860. The arrival of U.S. Army troops ended this so-called Pyramid Lake War.

Soon afterward a different group of Nevada Indians, the Western Shoshone, signed a treaty with the U.S. government at Ruby Valley, in northeastern Nevada. For twenty years the California Trail had passed near the valley, and the U.S. Army had established a fort there in 1862. The following year the treaty was signed. The Western Shoshone, who had often lived and hunted in the valley during wintertime, gave many rights over Ruby Valley to the United States and also agreed to live on reservations if required to do so by the federal government. Although the signing was peaceful, the Shoshone people later claimed that the U.S. government had not lived up to the terms of the agreement. Legal arguments over the treaty are still going on.

In 1861 Congress took western Nevada away from Utah, naming it the Nevada Territory. Carson City, a town that had grown on the site of a pioneer trading post, was made Nevada's capital. Later in the 1860s, Congress would give Nevada additional territory from Utah and Arizona, creating what would become the state's present boundaries.

The Comstock brought overnight growth to western Nevada. By 1863 Virginia City had grown from a huddle of tents reached only by a burro track into the second most important town in the American West, after San Francisco. Lying at the center of a network of roads, it had an opera house, four banks, six churches—and 110 saloons and gambling halls.

The rising conflict over slavery in the United States led to the outbreak of the Civil War in 1861. The Nevada Territory supported the Northern, or Union, side, and President Abraham Lincoln was eager to make Nevada a state, partly as a reward for its loyalty and partly because doing so would add another free state to the Senate vote on ending slavery. He officially named Nevada the country's thirty-sixth

By the 1870s Virginia City had grown from a mining camp to an important center of commerce.

state on October 31, 1864. Nevada's first congressman and senators rushed to Washington, D.C., to cast vital votes for the Thirteenth Amendment, which abolished slavery. Less than six months later, when word of Lincoln's assassination reached Nevada, the streets of Virginia City were draped in black, the church bells tolled, and even the saloons closed for a day.

BOOM AND BUST

The hills around Virginia City were honeycombed with caverns and tunnels where men labored day and night, often in scorching heat, to claw the precious ore from its resting place. Conditions were very dangerous, even after an engineer named Philipp Deidesheimer invented square-set timbering, a method of joining timbers into hollow cubes to reinforce the tunnels on all sides. Like many others on the Comstock, Deidesheimer failed to make a fortune—he missed the chance to patent his invention, which was immediately adopted at all the mines.

The new method of shoring up the mines, combined with the constant construction of new buildings, created a ravenous appetite for timber, which had to be brought to the treeless Comstock from the slopes of the Sierra Nevada, more than 10 miles away. Hauling the logs in wagons was expensive and time consuming, so in 1867 loggers began using flumes to move timber to the mines. A flume was a shallow trough of wooden planks, partly filled with water from a mountain stream. Logs loaded into flumes in the mountains floated down over canyons and around hills to lumberyards far below. In 1875 a new 15-mile flume was built. The first things to travel down it were not logs but two little boats carrying lumber company officials and a reporter. The reporter later described the terrifying, bone-rattling ride: "You have nothing to hold to; you have only to sit still, take all the water that comes—drenching you like a plunge through the surf—and wait for eternity." Today, similar rides—although shorter and safer—are popular features at water parks.

In addition to statehood, the 1860s brought a revolution in transportation. The first railway across the West, completed in 1869, ran through north-central Nevada along the route once followed by wagon trains. Other, shorter lines followed, serving the mining region and linking it with other parts of the state.

"IN RAWHIDE"

You'll have a hard time finding the ghost town of Rawhide on the map today, but when this song was published in 1908, Rawhide was a gold boomtown. During the glory years of 1907 and 1908, an estimated ten thousand people swarmed into Mineral County. Most of the town was destroyed by a fire that raced through the tents and wooden buildings on September 4, 1908.

Words By Fred Jones

Music By Glenn W. Ashley

I've found a place up - on the face of this great
Now I am here, I'll tell you, dear, We'll have great that

des - ert land; That's win - ing name
lit - tle home We've talked a - bout,

by min - ing fame, From rock - y hill and sand.
but did with - out, Be - cause I had to roam.

Where young and old are find - ing gold; And
And we'll have gold when we are old; And

class no one de - fines. For near - ly
man - y plea - sures, too. So I'll be

As railroads spread through Nevada, towns sprang up along these new transportation routes. A good example of the link between railroad building and town building took place in the Truckee Meadows, a valley along the Truckee River east of the Sierra Nevada and north of Virginia City. The California Trail passed through the Meadows. At a

In 1869 workers cheered as the first train ran over the Sierra Nevada.

place called Lake's Crossing, a toll bridge spanned the Truckee River to link the trail with the route to Virginia City. In 1868 a railroad company laid tracks through the area, and Lake's Crossing began to grow into a town, which was renamed Reno in honor of Civil War general Jesse Lee Reno.

Three years later, Reno became the seat of government for Washoe County. As a major stop on the transcontinental railway that crossed the nation, and as a center of banking and shipping for the rich mining district to the south, Reno continued to gain importance in the new state. In 1885 the University of Nevada was moved from Elko—another town that had been born along a railway—to Reno.

For years the Comstock Lode dominated Nevada's growth and its economy. But the twenty-year boom, one of the richest in mining history, was followed by one of the biggest busts. By 1880 almost all the gold and silver had been stripped from the Comstock. Mining booms elsewhere in Nevada also went bust around the same time. People drifted away, and many of the rich, rowdy mining communities became ghost towns, empty wind-worn shells that gathered dust and tumbleweeds as they slowly crumbled. From a high of 62,000 in 1880, Nevada's population fell to around 42,000 in 1900.

The entire cycle started again in 1900, when a prospector hunting for his lost burro discovered silver in southwestern Nevada and established the mining town of Tonopah. Soon other miners struck gold nearby. The tiny town of Las Vegas was founded in the southern part of the state as a hub for railway lines to the new boomtowns. Within a few years, these mines had declined, but by then, Nevada was entering a new era.

MODERN NEVADA

As early as the 1850s, people began raising cattle and sheep in Nevada. Some were Mormon settlers who brought livestock from Utah. Others were California ranchers who wanted to take advantage of the growing market in the mining region. As the mining booms fizzled, some miners turned to ranching. The railroads helped, giving ranchers a way to get their livestock to market. But like mining, ranching had its ups and downs. An economic depression in the 1890s hurt many ranchers, but World War I (1914–1918) created greater demand for livestock, as nations bought huge quantities of food for their armies.

The Great Depression struck in 1929, eventually plunging the whole country into a dark cloud of unemployment and poverty. To improve their state's economy, Nevadans made gambling legal in 1931. By that time the state had already passed a law that made it easier for married couples to obtain divorces in Nevada than anywhere else in the United States. By 1909 Nevada had become the divorce headquarters of the United States. State legislators believed that people would come to Nevada to gamble as well as to get divorced, and that while in Nevada they would spend money in hotels, restaurants, and shops as well as in casinos. Although the divorce law later lost its importance as such laws became more liberal in other states, the gambling law laid the foundation for what eventually became Nevada's number-one industry. As soon as the law was passed, Californians streamed across the Sierra Nevada to Reno's first casinos. Not until the late 1940s, however, did gambling have a big impact on the Nevada economy. Divorce remained the main industry of Reno, the state's largest city, throughout the Depression.

The federal government fought the Depression with public works projects that employed thousands of people. One of the largest was the construction of Boulder Dam (now called Hoover Dam) in a narrow canyon of the Colorado River southeast of Las Vegas. A new community, Boulder City, was founded to house the dam workers. Both Las Vegas and Boulder City grew during the five-year construction project, which ended in 1936. The dam controlled flooding on the river, stored water for irrigation, and provided electricity by harvesting the power of water flowing through great wheels called turbines.

World War II (1939–1945) brought the world into the nuclear age when the United States dropped two atomic bombs on Japan to end the war in 1945. Although the atomic bomb was developed at a laboratory in New Mexico, after the war a large area of Nevada land was set aside as a test site for nuclear weapons. Such weapons are still tested there, although all tests have been conducted underground since 1963.

Nevada enjoyed a new boom after the war's end—a boom in tourism. In 1946 a New York gangster named Benjamin "Bugsy" Siegel opened a casino-hotel called the Flamingo, beginning Las Vegas's transformation

In the early 1930s, before Hoover Dam was built, workers had to dig huge diversion tunnels to carry the Colorado River's water around the dam site.

from just another desert town into a bustling, neon-lit place that some called Sin City and others called the Entertainment Capital of the World.

Nevada's population has grown a lot since 1970, largely due to its gambling and entertainment industries. The growth has been concentrated in the Reno and Las Vegas areas. These urban centers have had to deal with urban problems, including traffic congestion, air pollution, rising crime rates, gangs, and crowded schools, in addition to the water shortages that are an especially challenging problem in a desert state that suffers from frequent droughts.

POPULATION GROWTH: 1860–2000

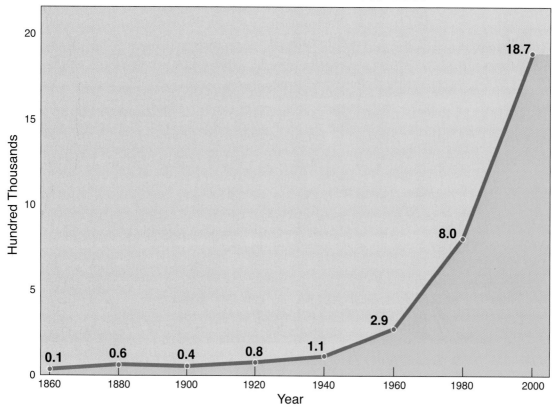

While many Nevadans were thrilled with their state's boom, they also recognized the need to plan and control growth. "This state's full of ghost towns," says an elderly man who has spent his entire life in southern Nevada. "We need to learn some lessons from the past. Don't build too high, too fast, because if the bottom ever falls out, you're in trouble for sure." Then he adds, "Still, people are never going to give up their fun. Vegas won't become another ghost town."

The bottom fell out for some people in 2007–2008, when the United States entered a recession, a prolonged period of slow economic growth and rising unemployment. Nevada was hard-hit by the recession. New houses stood empty or unfinished for lack of buyers, and some people who had bought houses were unable to make mortgage payments and lost them. Some of the state's fabled casinos went out of business. In October 2008 an article in the *Las Vegas Review-Journal* reported that since the beginning of 2007, Nevada's economy had declined more than that of any other state. Experts predicted that economic recovery would be a slow process, for Nevada as well as for the rest of the nation.

SHOWDOWN AT YUCCA MOUNTAIN

At the beginning of the twenty-first century, one of the hottest topics in Nevada was Yucca Mountain, where the federal government had planned to store the nation's radioactive waste.

The U.S. Department of Energy (DOE) oversees the nuclear power plants, weapons labs, and research facilities that use radioactive material such as uranium and plutonium. Contaminated radioactive waste—which is highly poisonous to living things—is piling up at those sites, and DOE officials have long wanted to move the waste to a single storage site where it can be monitored. The DOE planned to store the nuclear waste at Yucca Mountain, about 100 miles northwest of Las Vegas, on the federally owned Nellis Air Force Range. The plan was to put 77,000 tons of radioactive waste in rustproof containers in tunnels 1,000 feet below the mountain's surface.

Nevadans were divided on the Yucca Mountain Project (YMP). Some of them supported the project because it would bring jobs for construction, technical, and security workers. As many as 70 percent of Nevadans, however, did not want to see their state become the dumping-ground for the nation's radioactive waste. Critics of the YMP pointed out

Empty tunnels bore deep into Yucca Mountain, where the DOE hopes to store radioactive nuclear waste.

that Yucca Mountain has a history of volcanic and earthquake activity. The DOE, they said, cannot guarantee that movements in the earth will never cause radioactive leaks, contamination of the groundwater, or even explosions at the storage facility. And these dangers are not merely immediate threats. Nuclear waste remains radioactive for a very long time—spent, or used, nuclear fuel remains dangerous for tens of thousands of years.

The DOE, however, maintained for years that the site was safe. In 2002 the U.S. Congress approved the building of a nuclear waste repository at Yucca Mountain, and construction work began. By 2008 the DOE had applied to the nation's Nuclear Regulatory Commission for a license to store nuclear waste at YMP. Yet Nevadans' opposition to the YMP had not disappeared. The state's attorney general responded to the DOE by filing 229 challenges to its application, hoping to stall the project or kill it entirely. Pointing out that the DOE will have a big job to respond to all of the challenges, one state official said, "I do believe it's truly over."

During his campaign for the presidency in 2008, Barack Obama indicated that if he became president he would not support continuing the work on the facility. His victory in the election gave hope to those who had long fought to stop the YMP, including Senator Harry Reid of Nevada. In early 2009 Reid announced that President Obama would eliminate funding for the YMP. If this comes to pass, and the Yucca Mountain Project is really at an end, those who fought against the nuclear waste dump for thirty years will rejoice.

Chapter Three

Living in the Great Basin

"Nevada is a state that embraces contradictions, even thrives on them," exclaims Ron Dixon, a thirty-year resident of Reno. "We've got desert, but also Lake Tahoe, one of the most beautiful bodies of water in the world. We've got Las Vegas, the fastest-growing city in America, and we've also got ghost towns and some little towns that might turn into ghost towns. We've got recluses who live alone in shacks up in the mountains and come into town twice a year for supplies, and we've got celebrities and people from all over the world flocking to Vegas for big media events like boxing matches. But it's all Nevada."

GROWTH SPURT

In 1980 Nevada ranked forty-third out of the fifty states in population. By 1998 it had moved up to thirty-sixth. During the 1990s the state's population increased by more than 50 percent—the highest rate of increase in the country. "There are a lot of reasons to move here," says a newcomer who relocated from New York to Reno. "There's no state

For cow hands at Nevada's ranches, riding and roping are just part of a day's work.

income tax, housing prices are incredibly low, and the climate is great." Retirees, in particular, have found Nevada's warm weather and low cost of living agreeable.

Most of the growth is concentrated in and around Las Vegas. "The city's spreading like a rash in almost all directions," one longtime resident said in 2000. On a short drive out of Vegas in almost any direction, you could see mile after mile of new construction: town houses, apartment buildings, dozens of earth-toned, tile-roofed developments springing up almost overnight.

The growth spurt continued during the early years of the twenty-first century, with Nevada named year after year as the nation's fastest-growing state. In 2006, however, Nevada lost its hold on that title. That year Arizona knocked Nevada out of the top spot, according to the U.S. Census Bureau, which keeps track of population growth. Arizona's population increased by 3.6 percent, compared with Nevada's 3.5. Two years later, in 2008, Utah had become the fastest-growing state, and Nevada had fallen to sixth place, with a population increase of 1.8 percent. Why the slowdown? No one knows for sure, but some likely reasons are worries about a future water crisis and the fact that southern Nevada,

Las Vegas is one of the fastest growing cities in the United States, with up to five thousand new residents settling there every month.

POPULATION DENSITY

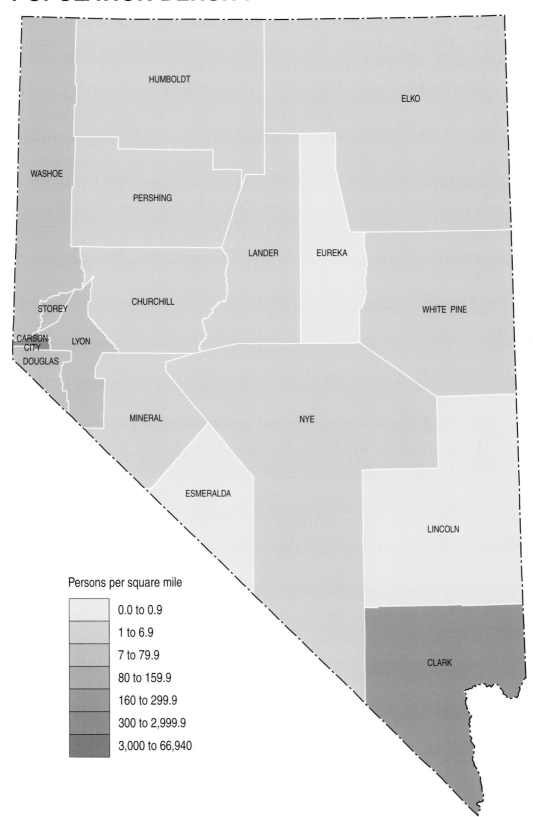

HUMBOLDT

ELKO

WASHOE

PERSHING

LANDER

EUREKA

WHITE PINE

STOREY

CHURCHILL

CARSON
CITY

LYON

DOUGLAS

MINERAL

NYE

ESMERALDA

LINCOLN

CLARK

Persons per square mile

0.0 to 0.9

1 to 6.9

7 to 79.9

80 to 159.9

160 to 299.9

300 to 2,999.9

3,000 to 66,940

the destination of most people who moved to the state, was becoming more crowded and a more costly place to live.

As a whole, though, Nevada is a more crowded and costly place to live. In 2008 the Census Bureau estimated Nevada's total population at 2,600,167, which meant that the state had 23.7 people for every square mile. That figure, called the population density, is low compared with the population of the United States overall—which is 84.5 people per square mile. Nevada ranked forty-second out of the fifty states in terms of population density, making it one of the nation's least crowded states. Yet according to the U.S. Census Bureau, Nevada is also one of the most urbanized states, with more than 90 percent of its population living in cities or towns.

BIG CITY, SMALL TOWN

Life in Nevada means many different things. Take Las Vegas. To a man from Mexico who works in a Vegas casino half of every year, the city represents opportunity. In six months he earns more than he would earn in a year south of the border, so he can take the rest of the year enjoying life with his family at home. "Maybe in a few years we will all come here to live and become Americans," says one Mexican worker. "Las Vegas is a good place for jobs." Fernando Moya works as a bellboy at one of the casino hotels on the Strip, the row of extravagant neon-lit pleasure palaces that defines the popular image of Las Vegas. He says, "I love Las Vegas. I love the people, the weather. But mainly it's the job."

Some people make the most of the city's economic boom while holding themselves apart from the Strip and all that it represents. "We operate totally outside the world of the casinos," says a father of three.

Antique shopping is a favorite pastime among local residents in the small town of Austin, Nevada.

"We just think of them as a blob of real estate downtown that we avoid with a passion." Seventeen-year-old Anya Margulies agrees. "It's like there are two cities here," she explains. "There's the Strip, the whole downtown. . . . It's really just for tourists. The real city, for people who live here, is hard to pin down. We hang out at different places and actually go out of town a lot."

Small towns, too, provoke a range of responses. "Wouldn't think of living anywhere else," says an elderly man who lives just outside tiny Austin, in the center of the state. "Life's just fine here. I know everyone, and everyone knows me." But small-town comfort can turn stifling. A thirteen-year-old girl from Tonopah, a town of about four thousand, complains, "This is the deadest place in the world. Imagine how bad it was before they had satellite dishes!"

Today the vast majority of Nevadans live in the urban areas around Las Vegas and Reno. Outside the cities, people are spread sparsely across the landscape. The federal government owns 85 percent of Nevada, in the form of national forests, wildlife refuges, one national park, Indian reservations, military sites such as the enormous Nellis Air Force Range, and vast tracts administered by the Bureau of Land Management (BLM). These lands have many uses—for example, ranchers graze livestock on BLM lands, and timber companies harvest trees from national forests—but they do not contain large towns. However, some Nevadans predict that if the state's population continues to grow, there will be increasing pressure for development of land that now lies quiet and empty under the desert sky.

ETHNIC NEVADA

Nevada has a long history of ethnic diversity. During the 1860s the United States received a wave of immigrants from other shores, and many of them came to Nevada, working in the mines or on ranches and railroads. By 1870 Nevada had a larger proportion of immigrants in its population than any other state.

Irish, German, and Italian workers came to toil in the Comstock mines. Later mining booms drew many Greek and Eastern European immigrants. One distinctive group was the Basques, a people from the Pyrenees Mountains between France and Spain. They had been sheepherders in their native land, and they came to Nevada to herd sheep. They settled in and around Reno, Winnemucca, and Elko.

All three cities still hold annual Basque festivals, and Basque-inspired foods such as garlicky lamb and stews prepared with salted cod appear on their restaurant menus.

Although the European immigrants encountered some discrimination, they eventually found acceptance within the general population. Nonwhite newcomers were not always so fortunate. Chinese immigrants arrived during the Comstock era to build railroads and work in the mines. Racial hostility against them remained strong in Nevada, as in other parts of the West, and by 1900 many of them had left the state.

Dancers celebrate the unique heritage of the Basque people who settled in Nevada.

ETHNIC NEVADA

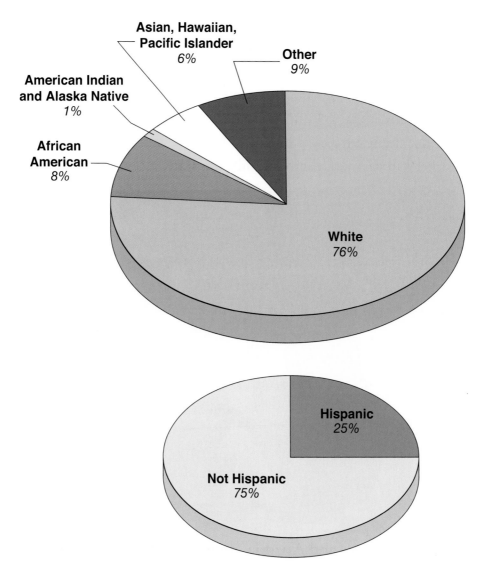

Asian, Hawaiian, Pacific Islander
6%

Other
9%

American Indian and Alaska Native
1%

African American
8%

White
76%

Hispanic
25%

Not Hispanic
75%

Note: A person of Cuban, Mexican, Puerto Rican, South or Central American, or other Spanish culture or origin, regardless of race, is defined as Hispanic.

African Americans had arrived in Nevada even earlier, during the period of fur trapping and exploration. James Beckwourth, a black mountain man, pioneered a pass from the Truckee River through the Sierra Nevada. Jacob Dodson accompanied Frémont's expeditions. Black rancher Ben Palmer settled in the Carson Valley in 1853; his family remained prominent in the valley for seventy years. Blacks entered Nevada during the mining booms, but in much smaller numbers than the European immigrants.

At the beginning of the twenty-first century, Nevada was still a predominantly white state. African Americans accounted for 8 percent of its population. The fastest-growing groups were Hispanic (25 percent) and Asian or Pacific Islander (6 percent). Many nonwhite Nevadans strive to find a balance between becoming part of mainstream Nevada society and maintaining their own cultural identity. Steven Kwon of Las Vegas's Asian Chamber of Commerce believes in the importance of ethnic ties, but also believes that Nevada's ethnic groups must see themselves as part of the larger whole. "We don't need a China Town or Korean Town. That's too isolated," he has said. "We Asian people are walking together with our community—the fastest-growing community."

Between 1980 and 1997, southern Nevada's population increased by about 300 percent. The area's Hispanic population, however, grew by more than 900 percent in the same period. Much of the increase was due to people who came from the neighboring states of California, New Mexico, and Arizona, drawn by affordable ways of life and jobs in the construction and casino industries. In addition, many came from Mexico, El Salvador, and other countries in Latin America.

This family is part of Nevada's large and fast-growing Hispanic population.

Many found that life in Nevada could be good. In 2006 nearly 6 percent of all businesses in the state were owned by Hispanics—a small percentage, but on the rise. Other members of the Hispanic community were happy to find employment with good wages and benefits in "El Pueblo de Las Vegas," the city of Las Vegas. The Soltelos, a Mexican couple who moved to Las Vegas from California, were thrilled to be able to pay for a new home, a minivan, and day care for their children with what they earned working at a casino and a restaurant. "It just proves that if you work hard here, you can make it," says Bernice Soltelo.

Nevada's Hispanic population includes U.S. citizens, foreigners living in the country legally, and undocumented, or illegal, immigrants. Most undocumented Hispanics, if they can find work, hold jobs at the low end of the pay scale. They work as day laborers, farm workers, or servants. Josephina Natera, a social worker with the Nevada Association of Latin Americans, points out that the undocumented Hispanics come to Nevada for the same reasons as those who arrive legally. They are "looking for a better life that's not often there."

NATIVE NEVADA

Nevada's smallest ethnic group is its American Indians, who total one percent of the state's population. Some of them live on the reservation lands owned by the various tribes. These include Duck Valley in the north, along the Idaho border, which has an enrolled population of about 2,300 Shoshone and Northern Paiutes; Pyramid Lake north of Reno, where about 1,700 Northern Paiutes live; Walker River in west-central Nevada, home to fewer than one thousand Northern Paiutes; Goshute, which stretches across the Utah border in the east and houses several hundred Shoshone people; and several smaller reservations with small populations, including the Washoe Reservation in Douglas County. About two-thirds of the state's American Indians, however, live off the reservations, mostly in the larger cities.

For more than 150 years, native Nevadans have struggled to define their role in the ever-changing place that was once theirs alone. When whites began settling Nevada, the Indians saw their way of life disrupted. Pushed to the margins of white society, native people explored different approaches to reclaiming their heritage and identity. Jack Wilson, a Nevada-born Northern Paiute raised by whites in the late nineteenth century, sought a spiritual solution, reviving a traditional ritual called the Ghost Dance, which Indians believed would link them to the powers of their ancestors and help them overpower the whites. Under the name Wovoka, he spread the Ghost Dance religion across the Great Plains in the 1880s.

During the 1880s Wovoka, also known as Jack Wilson, led the Ghost Dance movement to restore Indian traditions and power.

More recently, Nevada's American Indians have turned to other ways of winning legal and economic power. They have launched lawsuits to regain greater control of traditional lands and waters. They have also formed intertribal organizations so that different groups can act together on political issues. A. Brian Wallace, who served as chairman of the Washoe Tribe from 1990 to 2006, says, "Despite the many hardships that have been visited upon us in the past century and a half, we understand now, more than ever, the fierce urgency of today and the boundless hope of the future."

FESTIVALS AND FUN

For many Nevadans in pioneer days, culture consisted of a tattered newspaper or treasured book passed around a mining camp, and most

THE BURNING MAN

Nevada hosts many festivals that celebrate history, ethnic pride, or the arts. Perhaps the strangest is the Burning Man Festival, held in late summer or early fall in the Black Rock Desert in Nevada's northwestern corner.

The Burning Man tradition dates back to 1986, when a San Franciscan named Larry Harvey built an 8-foot wooden figure and burned it on a local beach, to the delight of a handful of friends and passersby. By 1988 the figure, now called Burning Man, was 30 feet tall, and two hundred attended the ceremonial burning. Two years later California authorities banned the burning, and the ceremony moved to the inhospitable Black Rock Desert, where it has continued to grow. These days, the festival attracts more than 15,000 people.

"Burning Man is about building a community and building art," says Hilary Perkins, who has attended three festivals. "Everyone becomes an artist." People come from all over the world to construct artworks that are ritually burned on the final night of the event. They also perform plays, dances, and operas, and construct distinctive buildings and costumes, such as a hut made of old bathtubs or a suit made of glowing flexible plastic tubes called light sticks. "They say extraterrestrials land in Nevada," Perkins laughs. "If so, they should come to Burning Man. They'd fit right in."

folks were too busy working to worry about recreation. Fortunately, times have changed.

Nevada's link with the performing arts stretches back to the lavish performances in Virginia City's opera house in the 1860s. Today, cultural events include symphony, opera, and ballet productions in Las Vegas and Reno, a Shakespeare festival at Sand Harbor, one of the West's largest art shows in Boulder City, and not one but two cowboy poetry gatherings each year. Las Vegas is the hub of all kinds of entertainment, including annual festivals of jazz, Latin music festivals, and casino shows by world-famous musicians and magicians.

Las Vegas is also home to some highly publicized sports events, especially big-ticket boxing. Nevada has no major-league professional sports teams, but the state's devotion to college basketball is legendary, and teams from the University of Nevada's Las Vegas and Reno campuses have loud, loyal followers. Reno also has a new AAA baseball team, the Aces. Plenty of other sports, some of them offbeat, take place in Nevada. A typical year's calendar might include golf tournaments, rodeos, shooting contests, balloon races, bike races, races on old-style, pump-operated railroad handcars, and even burro and camel races. And since it's Nevada, there's often heavy betting on the outcomes.

For those who want to be active, Nevada offers both highs and lows. The highs are the mountains. Western Nevada offers excellent skiing, especially around Lake Tahoe. "People don't always think of Nevada as the place for mountain adventures," says Jamie Weiss of San Francisco, who heads to Nevada each summer for a backpacking trip. "As a result, you can find some of the West's most uncrowded, unspoiled country here." The lows are the river canyons and deserts, which offer hiking, biking,

Nevadans eagerly follow college basketball.

and camping opportunities but require careful preparation to avoid the possibly deadly dangers of heat and thirst. As the early trappers, pioneers, and miners discovered, Nevada's landscape can be harsh—but to those who enter it with respect, that landscape offers magnificent scenery, solitude, and glimpses of a natural world that existed long before the busy streets and bright lights of the cities.

Chapter Four

Keeping Nevada on Track

The Silver State is still governed from Carson City, a city of 55,000 nestled below the tree-covered slopes of the Sierra Nevada. The dome of the capitol is sheathed in silvery fiberglass that flashes brilliantly in the Nevada sunshine—a fitting tribute to the state's first source of prosperity.

INSIDE GOVERNMENT

Nevada elects two senators and three representatives to the U.S. Congress in Washington, D.C. Closer to home, the state is governed under a constitution that was adopted in 1864 in Carson City. The state's government is modeled on the federal government, which has three branches that enforce, make, and interpret the laws.

Nevada's Capitol in Carson City, built in 1870, is the center of state government.

Executive

The executive branch of government is responsible for seeing that the state's laws are enforced. The six top executive branch officials are elected to four-year terms. The chief official is the governor, who oversees dozens of state boards, agencies, and departments concerned with education, environmental protection, economic development, health, and more.

Many sources say that Henry G. Blasdel became Nevada's first governor after statehood was granted on October 31, 1864. But Blasdel did not take office until December. The state's real first governor was James W. Nye, who had been the governor of the Nevada Territory and remained temporarily in charge of the new state at the request of President Abraham Lincoln. Nye's biggest job was to organize the elections in which the people of Nevada elected Blasdel as their new governor. Those same voters promptly chose Nye as one of their two U.S. senators to represent them in the federal government.

James W. Nye was Nevada's first temporary governor and one of its first two senators.

In addition to the governor, Nevada's executive branch has five other senior elected officials. The lieutenant governor stands ready to substitute for the governor if needed and serves as president of the state senate. The secretary of state supervises Nevada's business affairs, such as overseeing voter registration and the issuing of business licenses. The attorney general is the state's top lawyer, charged with representing Nevada in lawsuits and other legal matters. The treasurer manages the financial activities of state and local government, while the controller oversees the accounting systems that track such activities.

Legislative

The legislative branch of state government consists of two houses, the senate and the assembly. Voters elect twenty-one state senators to four-year terms and forty-two assembly members to two-year terms. These legislators make new laws and change existing ones. After both the senate and the assembly approve a proposal for a new law, called a bill,

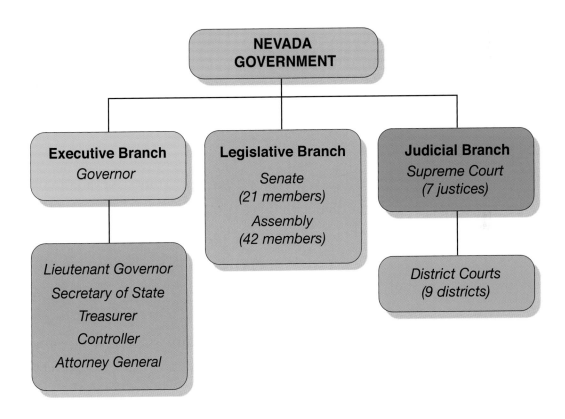

it goes to the governor. The governor either signs the bill, making it a law, or vetoes it, refusing to sign. A bill vetoed by the governor can still become law if two-thirds of both houses approve it again.

Judicial

The judicial branch consists of the court system, which is responsible for interpreting the law. On the bottom rung of the judicial ladder are municipal, small-claims, and local justice courts, where minor cases are heard. More serious cases go to the nine district courts. These courts also hear appeals from the lower courts, when one party in a case, dissatisfied with the lower court's decision, asks that the case be reviewed.

Nevada's highest court is its supreme court, which consists of seven justices elected to six-year terms. They review cases appealed from the district courts, and their chief responsibility is to determine whether those cases were properly tried under the laws set forth in Nevada's constitution.

POLITICS IN ACTION

One of the most pressing political issues for some Nevadans is environmental justice, the belief that no group should bear an unfair burden of damages brought about by pollution, economic development, or waste disposal. A question of environmental justice has pitted members of the Western Shoshone Tribe and conservation activists against the Bureau of Land Management (BLM) and a huge corporation. The scene of conflict is the picturesque Ruby Valley in northeastern Nevada.

Although Ruby Valley is not an American-Indian reservation today, it was recognized by the U.S. government in an 1863 treaty as part of the traditional homeland of the Western Shoshone people, and the Shoshone

The tranquil Ruby Valley lies at the heart of a political and environmental dispute.

have continued to regard the valley as the land of their ancestors. One site in the valley, Mount Tenabo, has special cultural and spiritual meaning. People go there to gather plants for traditional medicines on the mountain's slopes and to hold vision quests and prayer ceremonies. "I visit Mount Tenabo to pray to the Creator and to the life force of the world that resides in the mountain," says tribe member Kathleen Holly.

The riches that Mount Tenabo holds are not solely spiritual and cultural, however. There is gold in the mountain, and a Canadian company called Barrick, one of the world's largest operators of gold mines, wants to expand its nearby mining operation in order to get it out. For years the Western Shoshone opposed Barrick's plan for a cyanide heap leach gold mine on Mount Tenabo—an operation in which the poisonous chemical cyanide is sprayed over piles of earth and rock. The cyanide dissolves the gold in the piled material, allowing mine operators to remove it in liquid form. Many critics of this mining

NEVADA BY COUNTY

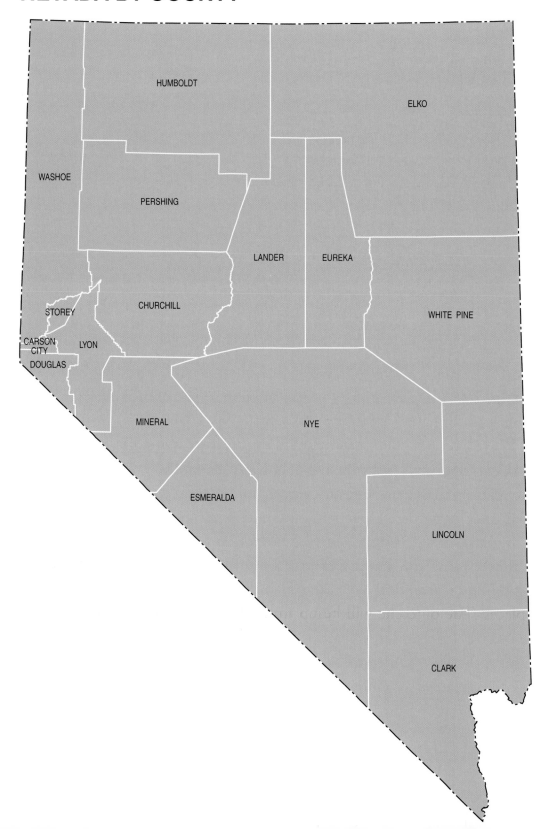

technique argue that it is unsafe for wildlife and people, and that it pollutes air, soil, and water.

In November 2008 the BLM, which administers the federal land on which Mount Tenabo stands, granted Barrick permission to proceed with the new mine. Five American-Indian and environmental groups promptly filed a lawsuit against the BLM, asking the court to cancel the permit. In addition, some Shoshone set up a camp at the site. They hope to block activities at the site, where bulldozers had already begun ripping trees from the ground, with their continued presence.

"The mining company and the Bureau of Land Management are trespassing on the Western Shoshone treaty land and are destroying our mountains, trees, food, medicine and leaving dirty polluted water ponds that are wide open making it unsafe to the birds and animals," declared a Western Shoshone member named Mary McCloud. On the other side of the issue, BLM official Gerald Smith said that the agency had followed all the required land-use laws and regulations in making its decision. And the president of Barrick's North American division said, "This is a vitally important achievement for Barrick and for the communities where we do business in Nevada," adding that the mine "creates new economic development and job opportunities in rural Nevada at a time when other industry projects in Nevada are being shelved and jobs are being lost."

As in many cases involving land use and resources, preservation of the environment collides with economics at Mount Tenabo. Added to the mix is the determination of an Indian tribe to preserve one of its sacred places. The outcome will be up to the lawmakers and the courts, faced with the challenge of balancing conflicting needs in a state where conflict over the land is an old story, and where 86 percent of the land is owned or managed by the federal government.

Chapter Five

Casinos, Cattle, and More

At the beginning of the twenty-first century, the tourism, entertainment, and gambling industry employed more than a third of all working Nevadans and produced half of the state's income. Nearly everyone who visits Nevada gambles—not just in Las Vegas and Reno but in small towns across the state. Casino communities such as Jackpot on the Idaho border, West Wendover on the Utah border, and Laughlin in the south near the California and Arizona borders let travelers gamble as soon as they enter Nevada. You don't even have to go into a casino: "The gas stations, drugstores, and laundromats in Nevada all have slot machines," one visitor from Oregon marveled.

The taxes on gambling establishments contribute greatly to Nevada's treasury, while the lure of casinos leads out-of-state visitors to spend

Today agriculture makes up just a tiny fraction of Nevada's economy, yet people still work in this resource-based industry.

money on restaurants, hotels, and other activities. In 2008 Las Vegas alone had about 37.5 million visitors in spite of the economic recession that gripped the country.

THE NUMBER-ONE INDUSTRY

Gambling has a long and checkered history in Nevada. Miners on the Comstock wagered and sometimes fought over high-stakes card games. Early gambling halls in the Reno–Tahoe area became the state's first casinos. In 1910 Nevada passed a law against gambling—but the practice didn't stop. Instead, gambling simply went underground. In 1931 Nevada made gambling legal once again. Phil Tobin, the state assemblyman who introduced the legalization, later said, "The state was practically broke but gambling wasn't contributing a cockeyed penny. I just wanted to see them pay their way. That way, we could pick up money from the license fees." During the 1940s and 1950s organized crime gangs controlled many of Las Vegas's casinos. In the 1960s the state moved to clean up the gambling industry by forming a commission to oversee it and by allowing businesses to invest in casinos.

The 1990s brought yet another change to Nevada's gambling scene, particularly in Las Vegas. Hoping to shed the city's image of sin and shady associations, some casino and hotel owners began wooing families, providing rides, shows, game arcades, and shops geared to Middle American folks and their kids. Although gambling is still Las Vegas's main business, 12 percent of the city's visitors are under the age of twenty-one. Late at night on the Strip, Vegas's casino-lined main boulevard, parents pushing strollers seem as numerous as stretch limos. Another public-relations move adopted by Nevada and other places

The average slot machine on the Strip generates $107 per day.

was the shift from the term "gambling," which is associated with risk, to "gaming," which sounds like fun.

Whether it is called gambling or gaming, the industry is the foundation of Nevada's economy. Yet some Nevadans are worried about its big role in the state's way of life. Nevada has begun to recognize that compulsive gambling can lead to problems such as bankruptcy, family troubles, crime, and even suicide. Posters in some of the casinos list the warning signs of problem gambling or the phone number of Gamblers Anonymous, a self-help organization for people who cannot control their gambling.

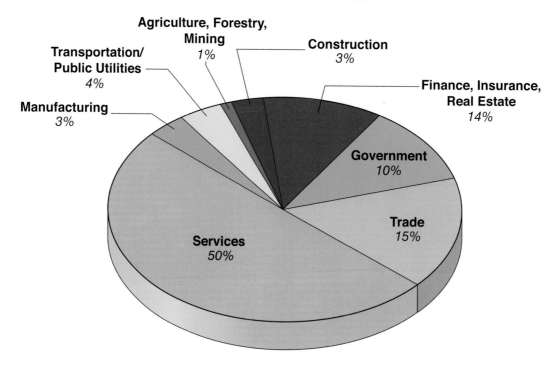

NEVADA WORKFORCE

Agriculture, Forestry, Mining
1%

Construction
3%

Transportation/
Public Utilities
4%

Finance, Insurance,
Real Estate
14%

Manufacturing
3%

Government
10%

Services
50%

Trade
15%

One challenge to the mainstay of Nevada's economy is the growth of gambling in other states. When the Las Vegas casino industry began, gambling was legal only in Nevada and New Jersey. Now some form of gambling is legal in all but two states, and casinos owned by American Indians have become top money earners in many parts of the country. Recognizing this problem, Las Vegas works hard to draw visitors by emphasizing its big-name entertainment and splashy architecture. One employee on the Strip explains it this way: "You can go to a casino on a reservation, or you can come to a whole city of casinos in Las Vegas."

Aside from tourism, Nevada's key industries are generally based on the land. Mining has always been important to Nevada's economy. Copper was mined throughout the 1970s, but by 1980 demand had fallen and the state's large copper mines had closed. Today minerals such as gypsum, molybdenum, barite, limestone, and sand and gravel are big business. Gold is mined with new technologies that allow mining companies to remove tiny amounts of metal from the massive heaps of low-grade ore discarded during earlier gold rushes. Silver, opals, and turquoise are also mined.

Gold mining in Nevada is a major industry, and one of the largest sources of gold in the world.

Ranching remains Nevada's leading agricultural activity, with the largest cattle and sheep spreads in the northern half of the state. Nevada farmers, many of whom depend on water from irrigation projects to turn their dry ground into productive fields, grow alfalfa, oats, hay, and barley for livestock feed. They also raise potatoes, onions, wheat, and—where enough water is available—corn, tomatoes, and grapes. "The future of Nevada's agricultural development," points out historian Russell R. Elliott, "as it has always been, is tied to the problem of adequate water. Nevada's supply is as limited as the possible solutions to the problem." Many solutions focus on using the water supply more efficiently, such as covering irrigation canals to keep water from evaporating under the hot sun.

2007 GROSS STATE PRODUCT: $127 Million

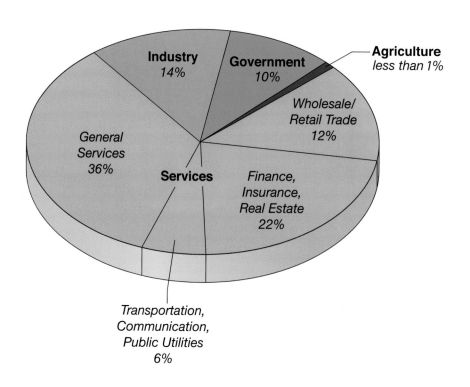

Industry 14%

Government 10%

Agriculture less than 1%

Wholesale/ Retail Trade 12%

General Services 36%

Services

Finance, Insurance, Real Estate 22%

Transportation, Communication, Public Utilities 6%

SILVER STATE BURGER

The restaurants and casinos of Las Vegas offer a dazzling variety of dishes from around the world. But if you want a real *Nevada* dish, try a first-class hamburger. You can cook these Nevada-style burgers on the stove, on an outdoor grill, or on a wood fire under the stars. (Have an adult help you with the cooking.)

Start with 1 pound of good-quality lean ground beef. Ground top round steak is the best. You'll also want four sourdough buns or Kaiser rolls. In a bowl, mix any combination of the following ingredients:

1 teaspoon each mustard powder, chili powder, and/or cayenne pepper
2 teaspoons chopped fresh parsley
1/2 teaspoon Worcestershire sauce or barbecue sauce

With clean hands, gently knead the seasoning mixture into the ground beef. Handle it just enough to mix the ingredients loosely—too much handling can make the meat tough. Divide the seasoned beef into four lumps and pat each one into a flattened burger. Cook them until they are hot all the way through and done to your liking. Serve your burgers on toasted rolls. Nevada farmers grow plenty of potatoes and onions, so have a side order of french fries, or top your burger with a slice of onion.

Since the 1960s Nevada has developed another key economic activity: warehousing, or storing goods for businesses based all over the country. Low-cost land and labor make it easy to build large warehouses in the state, and the network of railways and interstate highways means that goods can be shipped from Nevada to almost anywhere in the West within a few days. For a time, warehousing created several thousand new jobs statewide each year.

The growth of Internet businesses, in which someone with a computer in a cabin in Alaska can offer goods for the whole world to buy, brought a demand for Nevada's warehousing and shipping services.

Goods sold by Internet sales giant Amazon.com pass through this warehouse, one of many storage and shipping facilities in Nevada.

EARNING A LIVING

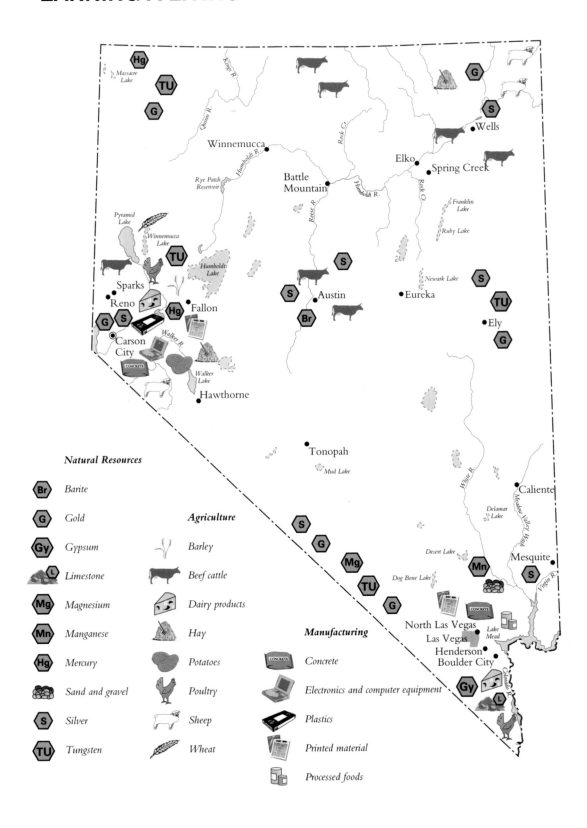

Massacre Lake

Quinn R.

Kings R.

Winnemucca

Humboldt R.

Rye Patch Reservoir

Rock Cr.

Elko
Spring Creek

Wells

Battle Mountain

Humboldt R.

Reese R.

Franklin Lake

Ruby Lake

Pyramid Lake

Winnemucca Lake

Humboldt Lake

Newark Lake

Sparks
Reno
Fallon

Austin

Eureka

Ely

Carson City

Walker R.

Walker Lake

Hawthorne

Tonopah

Mud Lake

White R.

Caliente

Delamar Lake

Mesquite

Desert Lake

Dog Bone Lake

Virgin R.

North Las Vegas
Las Vegas
Henderson
Boulder City

Lake Mead

Colorado R.

Natural Resources

Br	Barite
G	Gold
Gy	Gypsum
L	Limestone
Mg	Magnesium
Mn	Manganese
Hg	Mercury
	Sand and gravel
S	Silver
TU	Tungsten

Agriculture

Barley

Beef cattle

Dairy products

Hay

Potatoes

Poultry

Sheep

Wheat

Manufacturing

Concrete

Electronics and computer equipment

Plastics

Printed material

Processed foods

Solar panels such as these turn the state's abundant sunshine into marketable electricity.

Many retailers doing business in cyberspace found that Nevada is an economical place to carry out such real-world functions. In addition, business groups in Nevada worked to attract high-tech industries, such as computer-chip and software manufacturing.

The tourism business gave Nevada its second golden boom. The gold faded somewhat during the economic recession that began in 2007–2008. By late 2008 some casinos had gone out of business and Nevada's unemployment rate, the highest in the nation, had reached its highest point in twenty-three years: 7.1 percent. Governor Jim Gibbons and the Nevada legislature had to trim the state's budget by $1.2 billion because the amount of money flowing into the state treasury from taxes had fallen sharply. As Nevadans braced themselves for difficult economic times, some looked ahead to possible sources of future economic growth.

One promising prospect draws on two of Nevada's abundant natural resources: sunshine and wind. Both are renewable, and both can be harnessed to provide energy—something that people and industries continue to need, even in hard times. Entrepreneurs, environmentalists, and energy companies are joining forces to see whether solar power cells, windmill farms, and other renewable energy sources cannot only power Nevada into the future but give the state a valuable resource—electricity—that it can sell to other users. On the heels of mines and casinos, sunshine may prove to be Nevada's third big golden boom.

Chapter Six

Silver State Road Trip

"Nevada will surprise you" says Carla Druckerman of Pennsylvania, after touring the Silver State. "But if you want to see more than one side of the place, you've got to cover some ground." The state's tourism commission divides Nevada into six territories, each with attractions all its own.

INDIAN TERRITORY

Unlike the other five territories, Indian Territory has no specific location—it covers the entire state and includes not just the American-Indian reservations but also other places representing Indian life and culture, past and present.

In Overton, northeast of Las Vegas, the Lost City Museum of Archaeology explains the history and culture of the Anasazi. The Stewart Indian Museum in Carson City focuses on more recent Indian tribes. It houses a collection of arrowheads and other stone tools, with explanations of how they were made and used. The Nevada State

Mountain biking is a great way to explore the Cottonwood Valley Trail, one of several popular routes in the Red Rock Canyon National Conservation Area in Las Vegas.

An exhibit at the Lost City Museum in Overton re-creates an Anasazi pueblo now covered by Lake Mead.

Museum in Carson City houses an exhibit called "Under One Sky," in which the Northern Paiute, Western Shoshone, and Washoe people share their history and cultures.

If you visit Pyramid Lake, you will enter Indian Territory—literally. The lake is on a Paiute reservation. The northern part of the lake is closed to visitors, but you can view its southern shores from a scenic roadway or, with a permit, fish for its 40-pound trout.

Nevada's American Indians hold dozens of gatherings each year. Some are traditional religious celebrations, while others emphasize handicrafts, sports, or feasts. Many of these events, such as the Mother Earth Awakening Powwow held each spring in Carson City, are open to visitors. Most feature traditional music and dancing. The dancers wear dramatic fringed, beaded, and feathered costumes and headdresses. Some outfits, made of traditional materials, are shaded red and brown like the earth itself. Other outfits feature new materials, allowing the dancers to create swirling, exciting patterns in vivid colors such as hot pink and electric blue.

LAS VEGAS TERRITORY

Las Vegas Territory is the small but lively southern triangle of Nevada. "What can you say about Las Vegas?" sighed one travel writer. "It's impossible to sum up." Many books have been written about the city's attractions, which are constantly changing. By the early twenty-first century, massive theme resorts had begun to replace some of the older, more traditional neon-and-cocktail-lounge casinos. One such resort, the Luxor, has an Egyptian theme and is housed in a black glass structure that is the fourth-largest pyramid in the world. Paris Las Vegas is a huge hotel casino with its own Eiffel Tower (smaller than the original in Paris, France). The Venetian echoes the Italian city of Venice, right down to a canal that winds among its shops and restaurants. The scale of Las Vegas, though, is entirely American—the Venetian has more hotel rooms in a single building than there are in the entire city of Venice. These buildings contain hotel and meeting rooms, restaurants, and stores as well as the casinos themselves.

The casinos, though, are a world apart, especially the older ones. Generally smoky, they have no windows and seem to lack all connection with the outside world. "In here, under these lights, it's always eleven o'clock at night," an elderly woman chuckles as she works a row of the Golden Nugget's slot machines before breakfast. The constant electronic beeping and mechanical bonging of hundreds of slot machines drowns out the piped-in music. Some casinos, laid out in many branching chambers, feel like mazes. It's not always easy to find your way out.

These days, the casinos are only part of what Las Vegas offers. As you stroll along the Strip you can see circus acts, simulated volcanic explosions, or "actors in private battles." You can bungee jump, ride a roller coaster around an imitation New York City, or take a virtual-reality trip into space. You can stuff yourself satisfyingly and inexpensively at all-you-can-eat buffet restaurants—every casino has one.

Visitors to the Venetian Hotel in Las Vegas can ride Italian-style gondolas along artificial canals.

PLACES TO SEE

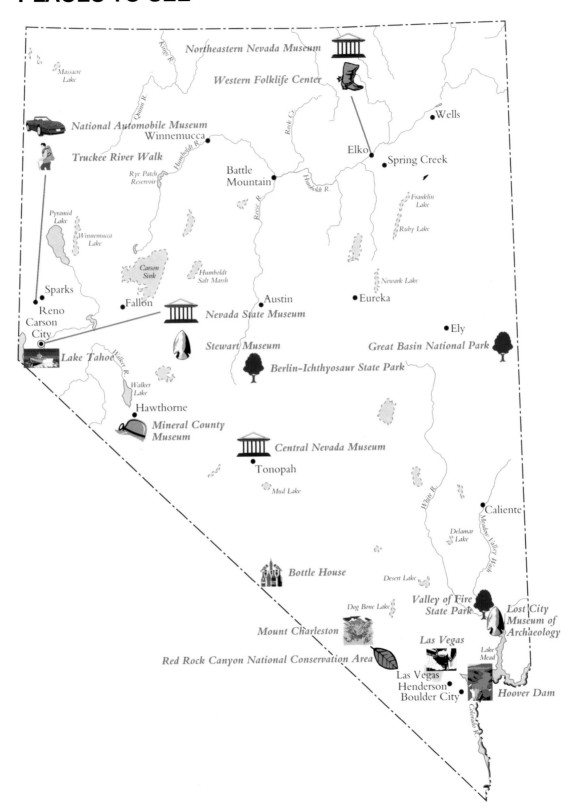

Massacre
Lake

Northeastern Nevada Museum

Western Folklife Center

•Wells

National Automobile Museum
Winnemucca

Truckee River Walk

Elko

•Spring Creek

Quinn R.

Humboldt R.

Rock Cr.

Franklin
Lake

Rye Patch
Reservoir

Battle
Mountain

Humboldt R.

Ruby Lake

Pyramid
Lake

Winnemucca
Lake

Reese R.

Carson
Sink

Humboldt
Salt Marsh

Newark Lake

Sparks

Fallon

Austin

Eureka

Reno
Carson
City

Nevada State Museum

•Ely

Lake Tahoe

Walker R.

Stewart Museum

Great Basin National Park

Berlin-Ichthyosaur State Park

Walker
Lake

Hawthorne

Mineral County
Museum

Central Nevada Museum

Tonopah

Mud Lake

White R.

•Caliente

Delamar
Lake

Meadow Valley Wash

Bottle House

Desert Lake

Valley of Fire
State Park

Dog Bone Lake

Mount Charleston

Lost City
Museum of
Archaeology

Las Vegas

Lake
Mead

Red Rock Canyon National Conservation Area

Las Vegas
Henderson
Boulder City

Hoover Dam

Colorado R.

Or you can get out of town and see some of southern Nevada's other sights. Hoover Dam remains as impressive now as when it was the world's biggest construction project. The Hard Hat Tour takes you deep inside the dam for a close-up look at its workings. Nearby, scenic roads wind along the shoreline of Lake Mead, a refreshing blue gem in a parched landscape. In the other direction, on Las Vegas's northwestern horizon, a tree-covered peak beckons. It is Mount Charleston, a cool oasis for picnicking, hiking, or camping. Just west of the city is the Red Rock Canyon National Conservation Area, a stretch of dramatic terrain that delights rock climbers, cyclists, and hikers. "I don't think I could stand to live in Las Vegas if this place weren't here," says Lauren Ganz, who rides her bike through the canyon three evenings a week. "It's the perfect medicine when I've had too much city and too many people."

PIONEER TERRITORY

Pioneer Territory covers a broad swath of south-central Nevada, from Walker Lake in the west to the Utah border in the east. Tonopah and Goldfield, the sites of big mining booms around 1900s, are located in Pioneer Territory. So are a fair number of Nevada's seven hundred or so ghost towns. While a few of these old settlements are run as tourist attractions, complete with restored buildings, restaurants, and motels, most have been left in a state of slow, gentle decay.

Many ghost towns consist of nothing more than a few crumbling walls, a dried-out well, and perhaps the traces of a long-vanished road. Some of the most remote ghost towns, seldom visited, don't even have names anymore. Others are better known for their unusual features.

Enormous hydroelectric generators may be viewed on a tour of Hoover Dam.

The Bottle House in Rhyolite incorporates about 30,000 empty bottles.

In 1908 Rhyolite was the second-largest city in Nevada, with hundreds of houses, saloons, and even an opera house. But the mines failed, and by 1914 only three hundred people remained. Today just a few structures survive, including the old railroad depot and the Bottle House, which miners built out of empty bottles.

At the northern edge of Pioneer Territory is Berlin-Ichthyosaur State Park. It includes the remains of the old silver-mining town of Berlin and a fossil dig where archaeologists have found the remains of ancient ichthyosaurs.

ON THE EXTRATERRESTRIAL HIGHWAY

For years rumors have flown about mysterious flying objects and lights in the night sky along State Highway 375, which runs through central Nevada along the northern edge of Nellis Air Force Range. Some people claim that the region is visited by aliens in UFOs, others say that the UFOs are really top-secret experimental military aircraft. Still others point to the lack of real evidence for any unusual happenings and say that the whole thing is nonsense.

Still, the rumors have attracted conspiracy buffs and curiosity seekers of all sorts for years. So many people were driving up and down State Highway 375 in the hope of spotting a UFO that Nevada officials decided to take advantage of the publicity. They designated the road the Extraterrestrial Highway and prepared brochures promoting it to tourists. The owners of an inn in Rachel, the only town along the highway, jumped into the act by renaming their place the Little A'Le'Inn (for "alien") and proclaiming "Extraterrestrials welcome!" The restaurant's gift shop sells a wide array of UFO-related merchandise, including T-shirts, keychains, and maps of the best viewing spots along the road. Are the people who visit the inn believers hoping to see a spaceship or skeptics who just want a good laugh? The inn's owners say it's about fifty-fifty.

You can learn about the ghost towns and the heritage of central Nevada at two museums. The Mineral County Museum in Hawthorne displays mining and railroad equipment from Nevada's early days, along with clothing, furniture, and other everyday possessions used by pioneers. The Central Nevada Museum in Tonopah focuses on mining and the boomtowns. Ore crushers and other huge pieces of old mining equipment dot the museum's grounds.

PONY EXPRESS TERRITORY

North of Pioneer Territory is Pony Express Territory, a strip of basin-and-range terrain that extends across the center of Nevada. U.S. Highway 50 runs through this part of Nevada along the route once taken by riders for the Pony Express and Overland Stage companies, the mail carriers of the Old West. Years ago *Life* magazine called Highway 50, which runs for several hundred miles through this wide-open, uncrowded region,

Today tourists can drive where Pony Express horses once galloped across the sagebrush, known as the Loneliest Road.

Stalactites by the thousands adorn Lehman Caves in Great Basin National Park.

"the Loneliest Road in America." The name stuck, and today at gas stations and cafés along the way visitors can buy souvenir T-shirts and bumper stickers that boast "I Survived the Loneliest Road."

The only national park entirely within the state of Nevada is located in Pony Express Territory. It is Great Basin National Park, one of the least crowded national parks in the country. "It's kind of out of the way, pretty far from any big city," explains Kathleen Worley, who grew up in Nevada. "You have to make an effort to get there, but it's well worth it." Great Basin surrounds Wheeler Peak, a massive mountain that rises majestically above the surrounding landscape. The glacier near the mountain's summit is the southernmost such ice formation in the United States. The park also includes the Lehman Caves, a magnificent underground treasure with some extremely rare rock formations. The flat, platelike shapes called shields occur in only a handful of other caves worldwide.

Austin, another small town on the highway, has only a few hundred inhabitants but contains many well-preserved buildings from the nineteenth century. The International Hotel, built in 1859 in Virginia City but moved to Austin in 1863, is believed to be Nevada's oldest hotel.

If you're driving on the Loneliest Road, you're bound to stop in Eureka, a tiny town that was once a lead-mining center. Eureka's centerpiece is its 1880 opera house, which has a magnificent painted curtain dating from 1924.

COWBOY COUNTRY

The northern third of Nevada is Cowboy Country. As its name suggests, this part of Nevada is where the state's ranching is concentrated. Horseback riding, roping, and other cowboy skills are still part of everyday life for many men and women. The city of Elko, once a stopover for wagon trains, is now the center of a movement to preserve and celebrate the area's heritage through events such as the Cowboy Poetry Gathering, the Basque Festival, and the Silver State Stampede Rodeo. Its Northeastern Nevada Museum has exhibits about local American-Indian, pioneer, mining, and ranching history as well as the area's wildlife. The Western Folklife Center is dedicated to preserving ranch culture, including handicrafts such as whittling, which is the art of carving shapes out of raw wood with a knife.

Thrill-seeking snowboarders are drawn to the Ruby Mountains in winter.

Cowboy Country also includes outdoor attractions. The Ruby Mountains, south of Elko, are the wettest and greenest range in Nevada. They attract hikers in the summertime, and in winter, skiers are airlifted in by helicopter to carve the powdery snow. Near the Rubies is glacier-carved Lamoille Canyon, where visitors can drive through a vista of dramatic stone peaks and cliffs.

RENO–TAHOE TERRITORY

Reno–Tahoe Territory runs up the western border of Nevada from Lake Tahoe to the Oregon border. The lake is one of Nevada's most beautiful sights, a deep gem of cool sapphire water backed by the forested slopes of the Sierra Nevada. Lake Tahoe has long been famed for its invigorating climate and bracing air. Author Mark Twain declared in the nineteenth century, "Three months of camp life on Lake Tahoe would restore an Egyptian mummy to his pristine vigor, and give him an appetite like an alligator." Summer boating, winter skiing on the surrounding mountains, and casinos along the shore make Lake Tahoe an all-purpose recreation center.

TEN LARGEST CITIES

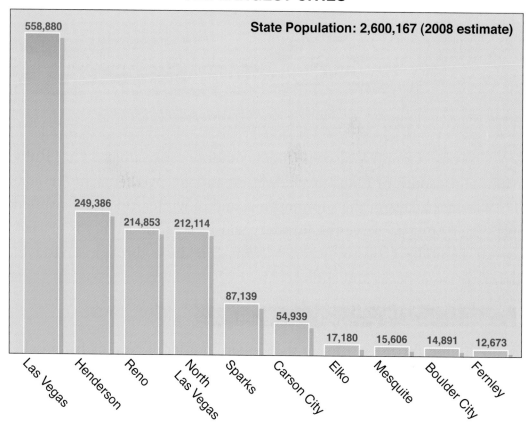

State Population: 2,600,167 (2008 estimate)

City	Population
Las Vegas	558,880
Henderson	249,386
Reno	214,853
North Las Vegas	212,114
Sparks	87,139
Carson City	54,939
Elko	17,180
Mesquite	15,606
Boulder City	14,891
Fernley	12,673

With 72 miles of shoreline and an average depth of 989 feet, Lake Tahoe is a cool blue gem among the peaks of the Sierra Nevada.

The Nevada State Railroad Museum preserves the railroad heritage of Nevada, including locomotives of the famous Virginia and Truckee Railroad.

Nine miles from the lake is Carson City, the state capital. Its premier attraction is the Nevada State Museum. Among the museum's holdings are baskets made by Washoe artist Dat-So-La-Lee. The nearby Nevada State Railroad Museum displays more than sixty pieces of train equipment from the Virginia and Truckee Railroad and other Nevada lines, which hauled ore from the Comstock mines. Some pieces still function, and visitors can take a short ride along a stretch of the old track.

Reno, which proudly calls itself the Biggest Little City in the World, is a major gambling center. Reno has other attractions, however. The Nevada Historical Society Museum, founded in 1904, is Nevada's oldest museum and contains a library of documents dating back to 1859. More than two hundred antique or rare cars are garaged in the National Automobile Museum, devoted to America's love affair with the automobile. One of Reno's most distinctive features is the Truckee River Walk, a decorative marble path along the Truckee River, which winds through the city.

North of Reno is Pyramid Lake, and still farther north is one of the emptiest corners of the state, a region of playas and dry mountain ranges, of unpaved roads and long, long stretches between towns. This austere region captures an essential part of Nevada's character. Fast-growing southern Nevada is "where the people and the power are," wrote author David Thomson, after exploring Nevada's highways and byways. "Yet all the rest of the state . . . to the last bit of the northwest corner, where there is not even one small place to name, is Nevada, too. And the emptiness is vital, even if it exists only as a warning or a signal to the bustling, expanding south."

THE FLAG: *The Nevada flag was designed in 1929 and modified in 1991. It has a cobalt blue background with a silver star between two branches of sagebrush in its upper-left corner. Above the star is a scroll bearing the words* Battle Born. *Below it is the name* Nevada.

THE SEAL: *The state seal contains a group of pictures symbolizing Nevada. In the foreground is a plow with sheaves of wheat, representing agriculture. In the center of the seal, a mine shaft, a train crossing a trestle, and a building with a smokestack represent Nevada industry. Behind them, the sun peaks out behind snowcapped mountains. Underneath these images is a scroll with the state motto,* "All for Our Country."

State Survey

Statehood: October 31, 1864

Origin of Name: *Nevada* is a Spanish word meaning "snowcapped"

Nicknames: Sagebrush State, Silver State, Battle Born State

Capital: Carson City

Motto: All for Our Country

Bird: Mountain bluebird

Animal: Desert bighorn sheep

Flower: Sagebrush

Trees: Single-leaf piñon, bristlecone pine

Fish: Lahontan cutthroat trout

Fossil: Ichthyosaur

Precious Stone: Virgin Valley black fire opal

Reptile: Desert tortoise

Rock: Sandstone

Metal: Silver

Mountain bluebird

Sagebrush

"HOME MEANS NEVADA"

The Nevada legislature adopted "Home Means Nevada" as the official state song on February 6, 1933.

GEOGRAPHY

Highest Point: 13,140 feet above sea level, at Boundary Peak

Lowest Point: 470 feet above sea level, on the Colorado River in Clark County

Area: 110,540 square miles

Greatest Distance North to South: 478 miles

Greatest Distance East to West: 318 miles

Bordering States: Oregon and Idaho to the north, California to the west and south, Arizona and Utah to the east

Hottest Recorded Temperature: 125 °F at Laughlin on June 29, 1994

Coldest Recorded Temperature: −50 °F at San Jacinto on January 8, 1937

Average Annual Precipitation: 7 inches

Major Rivers: Bruneau, Carson, Colorado, Humboldt, Jarbidge, Muddy, Owyhee, Truckee, Virgin, Walker

Major Lakes: Franklin, Lamoille, Liberty, Mead, Mohave, Pyramid, Ruby, Rye Patch Reservoir, Tahoe, Topaz, Walker

Trees: alder, aspen, bristlecone pine, chokecherry, cottonwood, fir, hemlock, juniper, spruce, willow

Wild Plants: cactus, creosote, greasewood, Joshua tree, mesquite, sagebrush, saltbrush, yucca

Animals: badger, beaver, bighorn sheep, coyote, desert tortoise, elk, garter snake, Gila monster, mink, mule deer, muskrat, mustang, porcupine, pronghorn antelope, raccoon, rattlesnake, red fox, skunk, tortoise, wild burro

Porcupine

Birds: eagle, falcon, grouse, mountain bluebird, owl, partridge, pelican, pheasant, quail, sage hen

Fish: bass, carp, catfish, crappie, trout

Endangered Animals: Ash Meadows Amargosa pupfish, Ash Meadows speckled dace, bonytail chub, Clover Valley speckled dace, cui-ui, Devils Hole pupfish, Hiko White River springfish, Independence Valley speckled dace, Moapa dace, Pahranagat roundtail chub, Pahrump poolfish, razorback sucker, Virgin River chub, Warm Springs pupfish, White River spinedace, White river springfish, woundfin

Ash Meadows speckled dace

Endangered Plants: Amargosa niterwort, steamboat buckwheat

TIMELINE

Nevada History

ca. 300 BCE–1150 CE Anasazi live in southwestern Nevada.

1600s Paiute, Shoshone, and Washoe Indians live in what will become Nevada.

1776 Francisco Garcés, a Spanish priest, possibly becomes the first European to pass through Nevada Territory.

1826 Mountain man Jedediah Smith crosses southern Nevada.

1843 John C. Frémont maps the Great Basin.

1848 Nevada becomes U.S. Territory under the Treaty of Guadalupe Hidalgo.

1859 Miners discover the Comstock Lode, bringing a rush of gold and silver prospectors to western Nevada.

1860 Comstock miners fight the Paiutes in the Pyramid Lake War.

1864 Nevada becomes the thirty-sixth state.

1868 The transcontinental railroad crosses Nevada.

1874 Pyramid Lake and Walker Indian reservations are created.

1880–1894 The Comstock Lode and other mines peter out; around 15,000 people leave Nevada.

1900 Silver is found at Tonopah and gold at Goldfield; mining revives.

1909 Nevada passes a law against gambling.

1931 Nevada makes gambling legal again.

1936 Boulder Dam, now known as Hoover Dam, is completed.

1951 The U.S. Atomic Energy Commission starts testing nuclear weapons in southern Nevada.

1963 The U.S. Supreme Court settles a dispute between Arizona, California, and Nevada over the use of the Colorado River.

1967 Nevada passes a law allowing corporations to own casinos.

1971 The Robert B. Griffith Water Project is completed, helping supply the Las Vegas area with water from Lake Mead.

1980 Nevada passes conservation laws to keep Lake Tahoe clean.

1983 Barbara Vucanovich becomes the first woman to represent Nevada in Congress.

1986 Great Basin National Park is created.

2002 Work begins on storage site for nuclear waste at Yucca Mountain.

2007 Water authorities launch plan for new intake pipes to draw water from shrunken Lake Mead.

2008 Legal challenges to Yucca Mountain nuclear storage site may end project.

ECONOMY

Agricultural Products: alfalfa, barley, cattle, chickens, corn, hay, hogs, horses, oats, potatoes, rye, sheep, wheat

Manufactured Products: concrete, food products, machinery, printed material

Natural Resources: barite, coal, copper, diatomite, gold, gypsum, iron, limestone, magnesium, manganese, mercury, molybdenum, oil, sand and gravel, silver, tungsten, uranium, zinc

Business and Trade: advertising, communication, entertainment, finance, gambling, insurance, real estate, tourism, transportation, warehousing, wholesale and retail trade

Wheat

Cowboy Poetry Gathering Cowpokes from around the country gather in Elko in January for a weeklong poetry jamboree. This celebration of Western culture features poetry readings, workshops, concerts, and art exhibits dedicated to the spirit of the open range.

Chariot Races Each January an ancient Roman sport is revived as horse-drawn chariots clatter around a racetrack in Wells. The night before, people place bets on their favorite teams.

Cinco de Mayo Every year on May 5, a Mexican national holiday, Las Vegas and Reno remember their Hispanic heritage with a weekend of Mexican food, music, and dancing.

National Basque Festival Elko's Basque community celebrates its history and culture with a weekend of traditional food, music, dancing, and sporting competitions in June.

Jim Butler Days Tonopah hosts the state mining championships during this July festival, named after the prospector who discovered silver there in 1900.

Lake Tahoe Shakespeare Festival at Sand Harbor In July and August, award-winning actors perform plays by William Shakespeare at Sand Harbor Beach State Park on the north shore of Lake Tahoe.

Spirit of Wovoka Days Powwow Yerington pays tribute to the Paiute mystic who launched the Ghost Dance movement during this August festival highlighting American-Indian arts, crafts, and dancing.

International Camel Races In 1959 a Virginia City paper printed a phony announcement about this wacky event—and later decided it was a good idea. Since then, camel jockeys from around the globe have been charging across the Nevada desert each September.

International Camel Races

Genoa Candy Dance More than 4,000 pounds of candy is sold each September at this popular small-town festival. Visitors can also shop for arts and crafts and socialize at the Saturday-night buffet dinner.

Professional Bull Riders Tour October brings forty-five of the world's best bull riders to Las Vegas, where they compete for the international title and a $1 million prize.

Nevada Day Celebration and Parade The last weekend in October, Carson City celebrates the day Nevada became a state with a huge parade, the 1864 Ball, where guests dance wearing the fashions of the times, and other festivities.

Fisherman's Holiday Derby Champion anglers compete to see who can catch the biggest cutthroat trout during this November event on Walker Lake near Hawthorne.

National Finals Rodeo

National Finals Rodeo Las Vegas hosts the world's biggest rodeo each
December with ten days of roping and riding performances by the
nation's top country and western musicians, and a Christmas gift
show where visitors can shop for Western wear.

STATE STARS

Andre Agassi (1970–   ), who was born in Las Vegas, grew up to
become one of the best tennis players of the 1990s. Agassi is one
of only five pros in the history of the game to win all four grand
slam titles, taking the crown at Wimbledon, the U.S. Open, the
Australian Open, and the French Open. Known for his bold playing
style, he surprised the world by making a spectacular comeback after
a three-year slump in the middle of the decade.

Andre Agassi

Phyllis Barber (1943–) is the author of many books about life in Nevada. Her 1992 book, *How I Got Cultured: A Nevada Memoir*, describes her childhood in Boulder City and Las Vegas.

Lucius Beebe (1902–1966) was a prolific writer and journalist who was known for his dashing style. In 1950 he moved from New York to Virginia City, where he bought the *Territorial Enterprise*, a newspaper that had fallen out of print. Under his direction, it soon became the most popular weekly in the West. Beebe was also a railroad buff, and he wrote many books on the subject, as well as articles for such widely read magazines as *Newsweek* and *Saturday Review*.

Walter van Tilburg Clark (1909–1971) was the author of many novels and short stories set in the American West. His best-known work, *The Ox-Bow Incident*, tells the story of a frontier lynching. *The City of Trembling Leaves*, published in 1945, takes place in Reno, where he lived for many years.

Walter van Tilburg Clark

Dat-So-La-Lee (c. 1835–1925) was a Washoe basket maker from western Nevada whose beautiful designs won national acclaim. Her baskets were so detailed and distinctive that her fame spread far beyond the Washoe Tribe, and many are on display in museums today.

Sarah Winnemucca Hopkins (c. 1844–1891) was an American-Indian tribal leader, lecturer, and writer who sought greater justice for the Paiutes. Born in Humboldt Sink, she spent part of her childhood with a white family, and she later served as a scout and interpreter for the U.S. Army. After dishonest government agents caused members of her tribe to lose their land, she called attention to their plight in her book, *Life Among the Paiutes: Their Wrongs and Claims.*

Howard Hughes

Howard Hughes (1905–1976) was an industrialist, an aviator, an aircraft designer, and one of the twentieth century's most eccentric billionaires. Hughes began buying Las Vegas casinos in 1966 and helped clear up the city's image as a place to visit and be entertained. He lived for several years in seclusion at Las Vegas's Desert Inn.

Will James (1892–1942) was a writer and a cowboy. He was also a drifter, and was arrested for cattle rustling in 1914 and spent fifteen months in the Nevada State Prison. After his release he lived on odd jobs until his first book, *Cowboys North and South*, earned him enough money to buy land in the Washoe Valley. James is best known for his 1925 book, *Smoky the Cowhorse*, which won a Newbery Medal for children's literature.

Velma Bronn Johnston (1912–1977), also known as "Wild Horse Annie," dedicated her life to the protection of the wild horses and burros that roam the American West. Johnston grew up on a ranch in Reno, where she developed a love for horses. When she learned that mustangs were being hunted down and slaughtered, she led a passionate campaign to save them. The story of her struggle is told in the children's book, *Mustang: Wild Spirit of the West*, by Marguerite Henry.

Velma Bronn Johnston

Jack Kramer (1921–   ) is widely regarded as one of the top tennis players of the twentieth century. An aggressive player with a powerful serve, he won U.S. national championships in 1946 and 1947, the British Open in 1947, and four U.S. doubles championships during his career. Kramer was born in Las Vegas.

Paul Laxalt (1922–2001), who was born in Reno, was elected Nevada's governor in 1966. During his term, he helped transform the state's gambling industry by promoting legislation to allow businesses to invest in casinos. Laxalt was elected to the U.S. Senate in 1974. A close friend of President Ronald Reagan, he advised him during his 1976 and 1980 election campaigns.

Paul Laxalt

Robert Laxalt (1961–   ), is a writer who brings to life the experience of Basque settlers in the American West. Laxalt grew up in Carson City and currently teaches at the University of Nevada in Reno. His best-known works include *Sweet Promised Land* and *The Basque Hotel.* (He and Paul Laxalt were brothers.)

Greg LeMond (1961–   ), a champion cyclist, moved to Reno with his family when he was eight years old. He began winning bicycle races as a teenager, and he later moved to Europe to become a professional racer. In 1986 LeMond became the first American to win the Tour de France, the most famous bicycle race in the world. Shortly afterward, he was badly injured in a hunting accident, but he persevered and won the Tour de France twice more before retiring in 1994.

Liberace (1919–1987), born Wladziu Valentino Liberace, was a pianist who became famous for his glittering costumes and flamboyant style. Liberace learned piano when he was young and soloed with the Chicago Symphony in 1940. Through his television show in the 1950s be became a national celebrity. Liberace's act grew more popular—and more extravagant—with each passing decade. In the 1970s and 1980s he was a regular performer at the grandest of the Las Vegas hotels.

Liberace

Greg LeMond

Patrick McCarran (1871–1954), a native of Reno, served as a Nevada assemblyman and as a state supreme court justice before being elected to the U.S. Senate in 1932. During his twenty-two-year stint in Congress, he worked hard to protect Nevada's economy, and as chairman of the Judiciary Committee, he played an important role in national politics. McCarran helped create the Federal Aviation Administration and was a sponsor of the Internal Security Act, which he believed would help protect the country against communism.

Patrick McCarran

Lute Pease (1869–1963), who was born in Winnemucca, sought his fortune in ranching, mining, and hotel keeping before becoming a political cartoonist for the *Newark Evening News*. In 1949 Pease won a Pulitzer Prize for a cartoon about a coal strike started by the United Mine Workers Union.

Edna Purviance (1896–1958), a film star from the silent era, was born in Paradise Valley and grew up in Lovelock. While working in San Francisco, she caught the eye of actor and filmmaker Charlie Chaplin. Purviance got her first role in Chaplin's 1915 movie, *A Night Out*. She then lit up the screen in nearly forty more of his motion pictures, including such classics of the silent era as *The Champion*, *The Tramp*, and *Easy Street*.

Edna Purviance

Benjamin "Bugsy" Siegel
(1906–1947) brought opulence
to Las Vegas gambling. Siegel
ran bootlegging, gambling,
smuggling, blackmail, and
murder-for-hire rackets in New
York and California before
realizing his dream of creating a
gambling empire in the Nevada
desert. In 1946 he built the
Flamingo Hotel and Casino in
Las Vegas, cheating his partners
in the process. Six months later
he was gunned down in his
Beverly Hills home.

Benjamin "Bugsy" Siegel

George Wingfield (1876–1959) was a mining magnate who played
a major role in Nevada politics during the early twentieth century.
Wingfield owned twelve Nevada banks in the 1920s, and when they
collapsed during the Great Depression, the state was almost ruined.
He was widely recognized as the "boss" of the Nevada Republican
Party from 1910 to 1932.

Emma Wixom (1859–1940), the daughter of a physician from Austin,
became an internationally celebrated opera star. As a young girl,
Emma was a naturally gifted singer who would spend hours in
the open fields studying the songs of birds. After her first public

concert in 1879, she performed across Europe and the United States under the stage name Emma Nevada.

Wovoka (c. 1856–1932), also known as Jack Wilson, was a Paiute mystic whose visions inspired an American-Indian religious revival known as the Ghost Dance movement near the end of the nineteenth century. Wovoka dreamed that the era of the white man was coming to an end and that the land would belong to the Indians once again. Wovoka's movement ended tragically when many of its followers were killed by U.S. troops at Wounded Knee, South Dakota.

Emma Wixom

William Wright (1829–1898), also known as Dan De Quille, was nineteenth-century Nevada's most popular writer. An East Coast native, he was drawn to Nevada by stories of the Comstock Lode. De Quille edited Virginia City's *Territorial Enterprise* on and off for more than thirty years, presenting vivid accounts of life around the mines. During that time, he trained a young reporter named Samuel Clemens, who went on to international stardom as the author Mark Twain.

Valley of Fire State Park (Overton) Weird rock formations shape the landscape of Nevada's largest state park. Some rock walls are covered with petroglyphs—drawings carved into the rock by American Indians long ago.

Hoover Dam (Boulder City) Seven million tons of concrete went into the construction of this landmark, completed in 1936 to harness the power of the Colorado River.

Lake Tahoe State Park (Sand Harbor) Beautiful Lake Tahoe lies nestled in a valley of the Sierra Nevada. At Lake Tahoe State Park, you can camp along its shores.

Valley of Fire State Park

Imperial Palace Auto Museum

Buckaroo Hall of Fame (Winnemucca) The lives of legendary local ranchers are illustrated through stories and photographs as well as lariats and saddles.

Ruby Mountains (Elko) Hiking, hunting, and camping are popular activities in this scenic region.

Imperial Palace Auto Museum (Las Vegas) More than two hundred antique and custom cars are on display at this vast museum, including vehicles once owned by movie star Marilyn Monroe and singer Elvis Presley.

Southern Nevada Zoological-Botanical Park (Las Vegas) Animals and plants from near and far take center stage at Nevada's largest zoo.

Lied Discovery Children's Museum (Las Vegas) Visitors can learn about sound waves, monitor the weather, and even host their own radio shows at this interactive museum.

Great Basin National Park (Baker) Trails take hikers up Wheeler Peak, to the fascinating Lehman Caves, or through bristlecone pine forests with trees three thousand years old.

Great Basin National Park

Liberace Museum

Nevada Northern Railway Museum (Ely) At the former headquarters of the Nevada Northern, you can take a steam-powered locomotive past a ghost town or along a railway line made for hauling ore.

Liberace Museum (Las Vegas) Las Vegas performer Liberace was in love with glitter. Some of his most dazzling possessions are on display here, from a rhinestone-studded Mercedes-Benz to a grand piano covered with mirrored tiles.

Nevada State Museum

Nevada State Museum (Carson City) This museum in the former U.S.
Mint boasts a working coin press, a woolly mammoth exhibit, and
works by famed basket maker Dat-So-La-Lee.

Rhyolite In its heyday in the early twentieth century, the gold mining
town of Rhyolite had more than fifty saloons, three newspapers,
and an opera house. Today it's a ghost town, and only a few
desolate buildings remain, most famously the Bottle House, which
was constructed almost entirely out of empty bottles.

Nevada Historical Society (Reno) Located on the campus of the University of Nevada, Reno, the Historical Society offers programs and exhibits ranging from lectures and films to art shows.

Lake Mead (Boulder City) This enormous reservoir was created when Hoover Dam was built in the 1930s. Nevadans flock to its cool waters to enjoy swimming, fishing, and boating.

Berlin-Ichthyosaur State Park (Gabbs) Visitors can explore the ruins of an abandoned silver-mining town at this state park.

Stewart Indian Museum (Carson City) Baskets, pottery, and other American-Indian arts are housed in the former Stewart Indian School.

Berlin-Ichthyosaur State Park

Death Valley National Park (Beatty) One of the country's most dramatic landscapes, this valley of shifting sands lies in Nevada and California.

Lamoille Canyon (Elko) This dramatic gorge in the Ruby Mountains was formed by glaciers during the last Ice Age.

Northeastern Nevada Museum (Elko) Nevada history comes to life in exhibits on American-Indian culture, ranching and mining life, and the experience of the area's Basque settlers.

Death Valley National Park

FUN FACTS

The longest Morse code message ever sent was the Nevada state constitution. It was transmitted from Carson City to Washington, D.C., in 1864.

Hoover Dam contains enough concrete to pave a two-lane highway from San Francisco, California, to New York, New York.

In 1999 Nevada had 205,726 slot machines, about one for every ten residents of the state.

The nation's only round courthouse is located in Pershing County, Nevada.

Find Out More

If you would like to learn more about Nevada, look in your school library, local library, or bookstore. You can also surf the Internet. Here are some resources to help you begin your search.

GENERAL STATE BOOK

Williams, Suzanne. *Nevada*. New York: Children's Press, 2009.

BOOKS ABOUT NEVADA PEOPLE, PLACES, AND HISTORY

Aldridge, Rebecca. *The Hoover Dam*. New York: Chelsea House, 2009.

Hamilton, John. *Death Valley National Park*. Edina, MN: ABDO & Daughters, 2008.

Mann, Elizabeth. *Hoover Dam: The Story of Hard Times, Tough People, and the Taming of a Wild River*. New York: Mikaya Press, 2006.

Peters, Jonathan. *Springs in the Desert: A Kid's History of Las Vegas*. Las Vegas, NV: Stephens Press, 2007.

DVDS

Discoveries America: Nevada. Bennett-Watt Productions.

Haunted History: Haunted Nevada. A&E Productions.

Modern Times Wonders: Hoover Dam & Lake Mead. Travel Video Store.

Nature Parks: Death Valley. Travel Video Store.

Wild Secrets of Nevada. CustomFix.

WEBSITES

Native Nevada Classroom
www.unr.edu/nnap/NT/nt_main.htm
Developed by the University of Nevada, Reno, this site offers an overview of information about the American-Indian peoples of Nevada and their traditional cultures.

Nevada Information
www.nv.gov/new_KidsHomework.htm
Part of the state's official website, this page was designed to help kids with homework assignments, and contains a wealth of facts about the state, as well as links to sites about its history.

Nevada State Museum
www.springspreserve.org/html/nsm.html
This site is a guide to the state museum, which focuses on the history of southern Nevada, from dinosaur fossils to contemporary Las Vegas.

State of Nevada Official Website

www.nv.gov/

This site features facts about the state's government, economy, and tourism opportunities.

Virtual Tours of Nevada

http://nevadaculture.org/

Nevada's Department of Cultural Affairs maintains this website, which offers online tours of several of the state's art museums, as well as of geographic wonders such as Valley of Fire State Park.

Women in Nevada History

http://nevadaculture.org/nsla/index.php?option=com_content&task=view&id=658&Itemid=95

This part of the State Library and Archives website features articles about women who have played important roles in Nevada's history, past and present.

Index

Page numbers in **boldface** are illustrations and charts.

ABOUT THE AUTHOR

Rebecca Stefoff is the author of many books for young readers, including several in the Celebrate the States series. One of her favorite pastimes is setting out from her home in Portland, Oregon, to explore the West's back roads and hiking trails. She has enjoyed varied experiences in Nevada, from cave tours to weekends in booming Las Vegas to quiet trips across the state on the Loneliest Road.